Trump's Bananas Republic

Wayne Madsen

©2018 by Wayne Madsen. All rights reserved.

ISBN: 9780359077830

First printing edition 2018

WayneMadsenReport.com
with VonStauffenberg.org
P.O. Box 4232
Washington, DC 20044-4232

*To the Resistance against Trumpism, fascism, neo-Nazism,
neo-Confederacy racism, vulture capitalism, boorish
sexism, and just plain bad manners*

Contents

Introduction 5
Donald Trump: Nobel Peace Prize Laureate? 13
The Donald Trump Administration: "You finally did it, you maniacs!" 25
Donald Trump: a pariah and a threat to world peace 46
Donald "Twitler" and his Restless Twitter Finger 77
"It Can't Happen Here?" It damned well did happen here! 84
GOP: From the Party of Lincoln to the Party of Grifters, Flat Earthers, Flim-Flam Artists, and Shysters 109
Hashtag #TFA (Twenty-fifth Amendment) 144
Trump's 2 Million Minutes of Hate 154
There's a "fucking moron" in the Oval Office 166
The Insulter-in-Chief 178
Hurricane Trump 190
Trump's Twilight Zone 202
Index 214

Introduction

Donald Trump first barged into the living rooms of America on his reality television show, *The Apprentice*, which was followed by an equally-campy spin-off, *Celebrity Apprentice*. For those Americans who were more concerned about issues of war and peace, extreme poverty, lack of adequate health care for many Americans, and an environment being increasingly degraded by corporate polluters and ill-thought power generation methods, watching any reality television program was a complete waste of quality time. This was especially the case with Trump's two offerings for the ignoramuses of America. Why any sane individual would want to participate in a bizarre version of *Let's Make a Deal* and work for a misogynistic boor who demanded complete fealty does not say much about those who allowed these two programs to gain favorable ratings.

What person who deals with the daily reality of tending to gunshot wound victims in trauma centers, educating children with inadequate teaching tools, working three part-time jobs to make ends meet, or caring for the elderly in decrepit nursing homes needs a television show to understand the realities of life? Trump's world of vapid high-rollers in Manhattan, highlighted by his two dumb reality shows, could not have been further from the concerns of Main Street America. *The Apprentice* and *Celebrity Apprentice* were merely game shows with a sub-par emcee. If the United States wanted to elect a game show host as president of the United States, there were other viable candidates who, at least, could construct a simple sentence, be respectful of all the citizenry, avoid racist dog whistles, refrain from gas lighting political opponents, and not constantly shout like some second-rate carnival barker.

If America wanted a game show host as president, at least they could have elected someone like Drew Carey, host of *The Price Is Right*. As a former U.S. Marine Corps Sergeant, Carey know more about being Commander-in-Chief in his little toe than Trump could pack below his hair-weaved scalp.

Donald Trump has never been successful in anything in life. He inherited his wealth from his Ku Klux Klan-loving father, Fred Trump, Sr., arrested in 1927 at a Klan rally in Queens, New York.  Trump's privately-held corporation, The Trump Organization, always owed money on its balance sheets, whether it was to mob-connected interests, Russian and Ukrainian oligarchs, or multinational banks. Trump's Mafia-linked casinos in Atlantic City all went out of business. And, as for Trump Steaks, Trump Vodka, Trump Ice (natural spring water), Trump University, and other Trump machinations, they went the way of the hula hoop, Pet Rocks, Cabbage Patch Dolls, and Silly Putty. In fact, Trump could repackage himself as a new Trump brand name product, "Silly Nutty." Just give him a smart phone and he will tweet the silliest and nuttiest garbage imaginable. It pays to be truthful in advertising.

Commented [WM2]:
Commented [WM3R2]:

America knew what it was in for with a Trump presidency after former California Republican Governor Arnold Schwarzenegger took over as the host of *The New Celebrity Apprentice* on NBC, just a few weeks before Trump's inauguration as president on January 20, 2017. "Donald J. Trump" was still listed on the show's closing credits as executive producer. Trump, saddled with issues of war and peace, offered a prayer to the National Prayer Breakfast in Washington, DC in February 2017: "I want to just pray for Arnold if we can, for those ratings, OK?" It is more than certain that most breakfast attendees took a long look at the bananas in their fruit bowls.

On March 4, 2017, Trump, who could not be bothered a bit about North Korea or the Middle East, tweeted, "Arnold Schwarzenegger isn't voluntarily leaving the Apprentice, he was fired by his bad (pathetic) ratings, not by me. Sad end to great show."

Great show? *My Mother the Car*, starring Jerry Van Dyke, was more entertaining and educational. Trump's preoccupation with his old television game show elicited a video response from Schwarzenegger, "Hey Donald, I have a great idea. Why don't we switch jobs? You take over TV since you're such an expert on ratings and I take over your job and then people can finally sleep comfortably again." Even though Schwarzenegger, a naturalized U.S. citizen from Austria, was barred, constitutionally, from serving as president, even "The Terminator" in the Oval Office would have been more reassuring as Commander-in-Chief than the failed game show host.

President "broken record" had to take, yet another, verbal swing at Schwarzenegger in December 2017 during a campaign speech in Pensacola, Florida. Trump told the crowd, "I can't believe that Arnold Schwarzenegger bombed so badly on *The Apprentice*, my poor beautiful show." Well, he was right about one thing. It was a "poor" show.

The initial term of Trump was marked by the type of back-and-forth name calling usually found in elementary school playgrounds, where one bully always goads others into fights. In this case, the bully happened to be President of the United States.

Perhaps what was more pathetic than Trump was some of his fanatic supporters. Now, one could be forgiven for believing Trump, the consummate snake oil salesman, during the 2016 campaign. Trump's rhetoric about being an agent of change and a producer of quality jobs fell on vulnerable ears among laid-off workers in America's Rust Belt. The Democrats screwed up by taking the traditionally-reliable union vote for granted and they were gobsmacked on November 8, 2016, as Michigan, Pennsylvania, Wisconsin, and Ohio fell into the Trump win column.

In mid-2018, many Trump voters despaired from "buyer's remorse." They knew they had been sold a rotten bill of goods by the man who tried to sell Trump bottled water as "Vermont spring water." The water was actually bottled in

New York. The Trump Organization's advertising billed the water as being "bottled at the source."

And, in a case of a one-two punch, America was saddled with a born-again evangelical nut case, Mike Pence, as one heart beat from the presidency. In 2002, then-Congressman Pence told *The Hill* newspaper that he never dines alone with any woman, other than his wife Karen. Pence calls his wife "mother." That sounds awfully like Norman Bates, played by Tony Perkins, in the 1960 Alfred Hitchcock macabre thriller, *Psycho*. What does Pence have in his attic at the Vice President's mansion at the Naval Observatory in Washington? Mother, is that you?

Speaking as the Vice President, Pence said he wanted the federal government's budget used to fund HIV/AIDS research and treatment to be diverted to the funding of gay conversion therapy. Pence is proof positive that gay conversion therapy has disastrous results. Just ask those in Indiana who know him and his wife Karen (nicknamed by Hoosiers "Commando Karen") about James Dobson's Focus of the Family-run therapy sessions, which specialize in taking gay men and women and turning them into straight couples.

The Dobson therapy treatment may have worn off by the time of Trump's election to the presidency in the wee hours of November 9, 2018. According to Michael Lewis's book, *The Fifth Risk: Undoing Democracy*, there was an uncomfortable moment between Mike and Karen Pence after Pennsylvania was called for Trump. According to the book, "Mike Pence went to kiss his wife, Karen, and she turned away from him. 'You got what you wanted, Mike,' she said. 'Now leave me alone.' She wouldn't so much as say hello to Trump."[1] Someone should get their money back from Dobson.

Speaking of gay couples, Trump, at a September 29, 2018 campaign rally in Wheeling, West Virginia, told his audience about his *Brokeback Mountain*, Korea-style, moment with North Korean dictator Kim Jong Un. Trump said, referring to preliminary negotiations with the North Korean leader, "I was really tough and so was he, and we went back and forth . . . And then we fell in love, OK? No, really, he wrote me beautiful letters, and they're great letters. We fell in love." Who knew Trump had an affectation for rotund younger Asian men?[2]

Then there were Trump's hate fests, held in mostly red states across the country. In at least two states where Trump held his rallies, it was discovered that some of the Trump "supporters" answered ads posted on Craigslist. One ad solicited paid actors to cheer Trump at an August 2017 rally in Phoenix, Arizona. The ad stated: "Several people needed for Trump rally to be held in Phoenix. Minorities especially desired to hold pro-Trump signs,

---

[1] Michael Lewis, *The Fifth Risk: Undoing Democracy*. New York, NY: W. W. Norton, Inc., 2018.

[2] John Bacon, "President Donald Trump on Kim Jong Un: 'We fell in love' over 'beautiful letters,'" *USA Today*, September 30, 2018.

cheer on command, and show diversity. Please reply with headshot and resume."

A similar Craigslist ad appeared in Nashville prior to a Trump rally in May 2018:

"Crowd On Demand Is looking for euthisatic [sic] people fill in the crowd at an event rally on May 29th. European heritage preferred, anyone enthusiastic about making America great again welcome."

It is not certain how many "euthisatic" white people answered the casting call in Nashville or the number of minorities who were willing to hold Trump signs in Phoenix, in return for cash.

What is known is that some of the more thoroughly vile Trumpistas seeded social media with allegations that paid "crisis actors" appeared on the scenes of horrible mass shootings in Orlando, Parkland, and Jacksonville, Florida; Las Vegas, Nevada; and Sutherland Springs and Santa Fe, Texas.

If you believe "we have no bananas," think again. Trump's Bananas Republic is totally bananas. So much so, Trump's

"Gentlemen, this man may talk like an idiot and look like an idiot. But don't let that fool you. He really is an idiot." — Groucho Marx

chief of staff, retired General John Kelly, called the Trump White House "Crazytown."

And this is not some ridiculous reality TV show. To paraphrase the opening dialogue from the science fiction television thriller, *The Outer Limits*, "There is something very wrong with your television set. Do not attempt to adjust the picture. Trump is controlling transmission. If he wishes to make it louder, he will shout even louder. If you wish to make it softer, forget about it. Trump controls the horizontal. Trump controls the vertical. He can roll the image, make it flutter. His comments are a constant blur, and never at crystal clarity. For the next two years, sit quietly, and Trump will control all that you see and hear. We repeat: there is something very wrong with your television set. You are participating in a bizarre living nightmare. You are experiencing the awe and mystery of a nauseating reality, which reaches from the inner mind to . . . *The Outer Limits*."

One of the most infuriating things about Trump was his tendency to say "everybody thinks" or "everyone says" before unloading a huge truck load of horse shit on the American people. The mainstream media called this "projecting" or "playing loose with the facts." It is a shame that the Federal Communications Commission disallows the word shit and its varied barnyard compound words from the airwaves.

Donald Trump: Nobel Peace Prize Laureate?

On May 9, 2018, Trump responded to a question about whether he thought he deserved the Nobel Peace Prize for arranging a summit meeting with North Korea's Kim Jong Un. Trump's response was, "Everyone thinks so, but I would never say it." Everyone believed Trump thought he should get the Nobel Peace Prize. It was not long before Trump's "bromance" with the North Korean leader that he referred to him as "little rocket man."

"Everyone" did not think that Trump was worthy of the award. Only a few Trumpistas in the U.S. House "Freedom Caucus" – Representatives Luke Messer (R-IN), Mark Meadows (R-NC), Steve King (R-IA), Marsha Blackburn (R-TN)[3], Diane Black (R-TN), Matt Gaetz (R-FL), Evan Jenkins (R-WV), Jim Renacci (R-OH), Drew Ferguson (R-GA), Pete Olson (R-TX), David McKinley (R-WV), Brian Babin (R-TX), Doug LaMaffa (R-CA), Scott DesJarlais (R-TN), Michael Burgess (R-TX), Ralph Norman (R-SC),[4] and Kevin Cramer (R-ND)[5]; House Delegate Amata Catherine Coleman

---

[3] Elected in November 2018 to the U.S. Senate.
[4] Norman thought he was being funny during a campaign debate before the Kiwanis Club of Rock Hill, South Carolina in September 2018. Making light of sexual assault charges being leveled against Supreme Court nominee Brett Kavanaugh, Norman said, "Did you all hear the latest breaking news from the Kavanaugh hearings? Ruth Bader Ginsburg came out that she was groped by Abraham Lincoln."
[5] Elected in November 2018 to the U.S. Senate.

Radewagen (R-American Samoa) -- and two members of the far-right and inaptly-named Progress Party of Norway: Per-Willy Amundsen and Christian Tybring-Gjedde.

So, in Trump's world, 17 far-right Republicans in the House, a House delegate who represents an American territory that receives the sort of U.S. colonial treatment befitting a virtual tuna fish cannery in the South Pacific, and two far-right Norwegians, who missed being a part of Nazi traitor Vidkun Quisling's government by 78 years, constitute "everyone."

No corrupt head of state is complete without a cast of scoundrels, con artists, and scalawags of all stripes. A perusal of the backgrounds of some of Trump's chief supporters in Congress reveals what amounts to a rogues' gallery of ne'er-do-wells of the lowest order.

We begin with the guy who believes Trump should have received the Nobel Peace Prize, Mr. Messer of Indiana. It was discovered that Messer's wife, Jennifer, received $580,000 in consulting fees from 2015 to 2917 from the Indianapolis suburban city of Fishers, even though the Messers resided in McLean, Virginia.

Mrs. Messer claimed her mother-in-law's address in Greensburg, Indiana as her in-state business address.6 Competing with Messer for chairman of the House GOP "Sleaze Caucus" was Matt Gaetz, who represents much of the Florida Panhandle. Gaetz portrays himself to the Bible-thumping voters of the Panhandle as a God-fearing conservative. However, even a partial glance at Gaetz's record reveals at least seven arrests for drunk driving and a reputed alternate gay life style. Gaetz's politically powerful father Florida State Senator Don Gaetz, ensured that none of the arrests led to prosecutions.

Matt Gaetz saw his political career launched when he became a legislative aide to Florida's Republican House Speaker Ray Sansom. Sansom, who succeeded Marco Rubio as Speaker, was pressured to hire Matt by the elder Gaetz. Sansom fired Gaetz twice due to his aide's DWI arrests and Gaetz's habit of speaking on behalf of the Speaker without clearing statements first with his boss.

Sansom represented Florida's 4th House district. In 2010, Sansom resigned after he was indicted on fraud and conspiracy charges by Leon County state prosecutor Willie Meggs. The Florida House's campaign to have Sansom resign over his alleged ethical violations was led by Don Gaetz, who then arranged to run his son Matt to fill the vacant 4th district seat in a special election. Matt Gaetz

---

[6] Brian Slodysko, "City pays wife of influential Indiana congressman $20K a month for consulting," *The Chicago Tribune*, May 11, 2017.

won and was easily re-elected in 2014 with no Democratic opponent. After Meggs was indicted, Florida prosecutors dropped all criminal charges against Sansom. However, the political damage to the former Florida House Speaker was done. Matt Gaetz and his father used the corrupt prosecutor-manufactured political grave of Sansom to launch Gaetz's current campaign for the U.S. House.

And what would be Panhandle politics without a dead body? One of Gaetz's three roommates at Florida State University in Tallahassee was reportedly found dead in 2004, under suspicious circumstances, while they were in their senior year. The same political machine that drove Sansom from office was used to cover up the circumstances of the roommate's death. Sources close to the investigation of the death revealed to this author that the Florida Department of Law Enforcement investigated the roommate's death as a possible homicide but the agency was politically-pressured by Don Gaetz and his allies to rule it a suicide. As with Gaetz's multiple DWIs, the suspicious death of his college roommate was buried by Florida authorities and the university.[7]

No wonder Gaetz came quickly to the defense of GOP Representative Jim Jordan (R-OH), a co-founder of the House "Freedom Caucus," after allegations surfaced at the Ohio State University that Jordan helped cover accusations of sexual abuse of members of Jordan's wrestling team by the university's doctor.

---

[7] Wayne Madsen, "Florida Panhandle's GOP politics: Sex, Lies, and Dead Bodies," WayneMadsenReport.com, August 26-28, 2016.

Gaetz advanced the elaborate conspiracy theory that the charges against Jordan were all part of some nefarious plot by the FBI and others to draw attention away from alleged FBI misconduct in investigating the Trump campaign and administration for colluding with foreign interests. No wonder Gaetz was invited a few times to fly to Florida aboard Air Force One with the chief conspiracy nut, Donald Trump.

 Wrestling team members should avoid "Full Nelson" moves by either Dennis Hastert or Jim "Gym" Jordan

Jordan was the assistant coach of the wrestling team. The charges against Jordan were reminiscent of those that led to the arrest and successful federal prosecution of former GOP U.S. House Speaker Dennis Hastert, who was making hush money payments to a male student who accused Hastert of molesting him while he was a member of Hastert's Yorkville (Illinois) High School wrestling team.

The charges made against Jordan, who had ambitions of succeeding Paul Ryan as Speaker of the House of Representatives, also reminded people of the cover-up by Penn State football coach Joe Paterno of sexual assault of football team members by his assistant coach, Jerry Sandusky. There's something about the post-Ronald Reagan Republican Party and it is the common thread of sexual assault by those in a position of authority and responsibility. Jordan, Hastert, Paterno, and others – all "bananas Republicans."

While we're on the subject of "bananas," another GOP congressman who believed Trump should be awarded the Nobel Peace Prize was Texas Representative Louis  Gohmert. In 2013, during testimony before the House Judiciary Committee, Gohmert said Attorney General Eric Holder not only questioned his integrity (as if he had any) but "cast aspersions on my asparagus."

Later, when questioned about his bizarre statement affected by a malapropism, Gohmert replied, "The expression 'casting aspersions on my asparagus' is something I found to be helpful in defusing heated exchanges during my days as a litigator, sometimes even bringing a smile from a frown at the thought of something so unexpected as asparagus during such an exchange . . .It has actually been amusing to see the national and international speculation as to what people think may have been the secret meaning."[8]

No, there was no "secret meaning," as much as Gohmert's delusional supporters might have believed. The actual meaning of Gohmert's ludicrous comment was that he was and remains crazier than a shithouse rat. Comedian Norm

---

[8] Gary Bass, "Gohmert's 'asparagus' making headlines," KLTV Channel 7, May 15, 2013.

Crosby was funny because of his malapropisms. Gohmert's malapropisms were due to his being just plain stupid.

Trump could always rely on Gohmert to have his back, front, and asparagus. In some cases, Republicans offer up a salad of bananas and asparagus. Sure, it sounds awful. But "bananas Republicans" are just plain awful.

As for Freedom Caucus chief Mark Meadows, Kenny West, his chief of staff, resigned in 2015 over allegations of inappropriate behavior toward female members of Meadows's staff. But rather than a total severance, as House rules require, Meadows kept West on his staff, between April and August 2015, at a cost of $58,125 to the taxpayers.[9]

Another House fan of awarding Trump a Nobel prize was Representative Scott DesJarlais of Tennessee. Where there was a Bible-thumping evangelical GOP congressman in the South, there was a guaranteed scandal. The day before election day in Louisiana in 1983, Democratic gubernatorial candidate Edwin Edwards joked, "The only way I can lose this election is if I'm caught in bed with either a dead girl or a live boy." The good news for DesJarlais, a physician, is that he wasn't caught in bed with a dead girl or live boy. He was, however, involved in an extramarital affair with a female patient. And, the "pro-life" Republican arranged for both his ex-wife and mistress to have abortions.

---

[9] Mary Troyan, "Ethics probe of Rep. Mark Meadows Continues," *USA Today*, August 17, 2016.

Iowa Representative Steve King was the closest thing to having a Grand Dragon of the Ku Klux Klan in Congress. King, who had a Confederate flag hanging in his House office, was fond of using the jargon of the white supremacist alt-right to go after people of color, Democrats, "liberals," non-white immigrants, and just about anybody that didn't fit into his notion of a lily-white country of pig roasts, square dances, and certain people "knowing their places." King once said on MS-NBC that white Europeans have contributed more to the world than any other "sub-group of people."

King, like Trump, was also fond of re-tweeting postings from British neo-Nazis. King had a fondness for Mark Collett, who had expressed his admiration for Adolf Hitler, while Trump liked the rantings of Paul Golding, a leader of the neo-Nazi Britain First organization.

On March 12, 2017, King tweeted: "We can't restore our civilization with somebody else's babies." King was a habitué of far-right political party conferences in Europe, where he felt right at home with such xenophobic politicians as Geert Wilders of the Dutch Freedom Party and the Austrian Freedom Party's leadership. King and his fellow Trump Nobel Prize cheerleader, Representative Marsha Blackburn of Tennessee, invited Austrian Freedom Party leader Heinz-Christian Sträche and the party's former presidential candidate, Norbert Hofer, to Trump's 2017 inauguration. There, they were able to rub shoulders with American xenophobic alt-right crazies like Steve Bannon and Sebastian Gorka, both of whom were given initial White House positions by Trump.

Although Bannon was Trump's chief strategist, no one ever figured out what job Gorka actually had, other than being a big fat bloviating asshole during television interviews.

A month before Bannon's, Miller's, and Gorka's pals staged their August 12, 2017 "Unite the Right" rally in Charlottesville, Virginia, the KKK held a preliminary rally in Charlottesville. For the Nazis and Klan, the Fourth of July celebrations had given way to the "Fourth Reich of July" tiki torch parades in which Nazis shouted, "Jews will not replace us!" What? Would Jews replace these vermin of society in neo-Nazi parades? Something about the advertising campaign associated with Trump's Nazis seemed a bit off.

Trump's "brain trust," consisting of his neo-Nazi speechwriter and special assistant Stephen Miller and "minister without a legitimate portfolio" Gorka, was complemented by outside support from Richard Spencer, the leader of the National Policy Institute, a white supremacist and neo-Nazi organization. Spencer re-located his headquarters from Whitefish, Montana to Alexandria, Virginia to be closer to Miller, a University of North Carolina classmate and political ally.

Miller and Gorka managed to gain the trust of Trump, who was impressed by the performance of both far-right staffers in televised confrontations with reporters. Gorka was irritated by the failure of some broadcast and print journalists to refer to him as "Dr. Gorka." In fact, the Budapest university that granted Gorka his PhD, Corvinus University, is the old Karl Marx University of Economic Sciences. In 1990, after the fall of the Communist government, a group of Hungarian academic con artists took over the facility and re-named it the University of Economics of Budapest. Gorka obtained his Master's degree from the post-communist university, which changed its name to Budapest University of Economic Sciences and Public Administration. The "university" offered MA and PhD diplomas to its students, but none of the degrees met even the thinnest standards of academic requirements.

In 2005, the "university" adopted its present name in honor of Hungarian king Matthias Corvinus. Corvinus only appears to excel in the field of agriculture, owing to its merger with the reputable University of Horticulture, which was formerly part of the Szent István University. At the Trump inaugural ball, Gorka wore a black tunic that sported a medal of the Hungarian nationalist order, *Vitezi Rend*. The organization was founded in 1920 by Hungarian leader Admiral Miklos Horthy, who served as the pro-Nazi Regent of Hungary during World War II and fancied himself as an "intellectual anti-Semite."

Corvinus's alumni list indicated the school's chief business came from granting degrees to Hungarian sports figures, fashion designers, entertainers, and aspiring politicians. Miller, a former staffer for Senator Jeff Sessions of Alabama, possessed neo-Nazi views that were horrific to his Jewish relatives. Miller called out CNN's Jim Acosta for being "cosmopolitan," a common Nazi reference to Jews. Miller also criticized Jewish poet Emma Lazarus's famous "The New Colossus" poem inscribed at the base of the Statue of Liberty. The passage refers to America's welcome to huddled masses of immigrants and refugees. At the very same time that Miller was criticizing Lazarus's poem, the

Nazi website "Stormfront" was referring to Lazarus as a "migrant-loving Jewess." Coincidence? Not when it comes to the re-emergent Nazi movement in America, which, instead of having heroes like Charles Lindbergh and Ezra Pound, as did their 1930s forbearers, followed icons like Bannon, Gorka, Miller, and above all, Donald Trump.

Wherever one looked in the Trump administration, they would find people whose heroes included, in addition to Lindbergh and Pound, Italian fascist dictator Benito Mussolini. During the 2016 campaign, Trump tweeted a quote of Mussolini, "It is better to live one day as a lion than 100 years as a sheep."

When asked by NBC News why he would quote a fascist dictator, Trump replied, "I know who said it. But what difference does it make if it's Mussolini or anybody else? I have almost 14 million people between Instagram, Facebook and Twitter, and all of that. We do interesting things, and I sent it out. And certainly, hey, it got your attention, didn't it?"

So long as something Trump said got the public's attention, that was the bar he set on what kind of malarkey he'd spout. That was not the mark of a leader but of a carnival barker.

No wonder former Vice President Joe Biden said one European leader told him, after viewing Trump shoving aside the prime minister of Montenegro to be in the front of a group of NATO leaders for a photo shoot, "All I could think of was Il Duce."[10]

---

[10] Ben Jacobs, "Joe Biden says European leader likened Trump to Mussolini," *The Guardian*, October 17, 2017.

The Donald Trump Administration: "You finally did it, you maniacs!"

In the final scene of the classic 1968 science fiction film, *Planet of the Apes*, Charlton Heston, playing time-travelling marooned astronaut George Taylor, discovers the remains of the Statue of Liberty on a beach. Heston's words became immortalized in the annals of filmdom: "You finally really did it. You maniacs! You blew it up! God damn you! God damn you all to hell!"

In the wee hours of November 8, 2016, shady businessman Donald J. Trump was declared the victor of the U.S. presidential election, garnering 304 electoral votes. America finally did it. They blew up the essential underpinnings of a democracy. It might have come as a surprise to the "prosperity gospel" evangelicals, whose political lodestar, Governor Mike Pence of Indiana, served as Trump's vice-presidential running mate, but in electing Trump, Americans damned themselves to hell.

The American people, fixated on inane reality TV shows, dependent on high fructose and carbohydrate diets, and brainwashed by Fox News, "finally did it." They blew up the country. God damn you all to hell, and that includes you, too, Mike Pence.

In the case of Trump hell, the very same Americans, who opposed the neo-conservative war and associated abuses of President George W. Bush, began to view the 43rd president in a bizarre and almost statesmanlike light. Who of sound mind and body could disagree with Bush's reported comments after Trump's January 20, 2017 swearing-in ceremony at the U.S. Capitol? Bush reportedly said of Trump's inaugural speech, "that was some weird shit." When someone like Bush 43 says he believed Trump was spewing forth some really "weird shit," you would have to be smoking some really "weird shit" to comprehend the statement and who said it.

Trump wasted no time in turning the United States into a Third World-style "kleptocracy." The United States was no longer what Abraham Lincoln described in his Gettysburg Address as a nation flourishing under a "government of the people, by the people, for the people," but a nation of cronies and grifters in high administration positions, all awash in foreign emoluments and payola from billionaire donors.

Trump was able to turn the United States into a virtual banana republic without barely a whimper from congressional Republicans. When the United States required someone like the fictional Senator Jefferson Smith, played by Jimmy Stewart in the 1939 film, *Mr. Smith Goes to Washington*, the country ended up with a Republican Party full of pathetically timid Casper

Milquetoasts. Senate Majority Leader Mitch McConnell, who bears an uncanny resemblance to "Bert," the "duck and cover" cartoon character from U.S. government Civil Defense television spots during the Cold War, only extended his shriveled face from his shell in order to veer away from Senate regular order and push through Trump's pro-big business Supreme Court choices, tax cuts for billionaires, and slicing and dicing of social safety net programs.

Republican House of Representatives Speaker Paul ("Eddie Munster") Ryan, who announced his retirement from politics on April 11, 2018, amid a challenge from a far-right "Freedom Caucus" led by some of the most perverted degenerates in modern politics – including totally "bananas" GOP Representatives Jim Jordan (R-Ohio), Matt Gaetz (R-Florida), and Louis Gohmert (R-Texas) -- had no spine when it came to the exercising of congressional power to block Trump's every whim. Trump stuck it right up Ryan's keister, when he announced tariffs that punished Harley-Davidson motorcycle company, which is headquartered in Ryan's home state of Wisconsin.

Not a single Republican and very damned few Democrats were willing to stand up a deliver the sort of speech the fictional Senator Smith delivered to a Senate full of scoundrels and ne'er-do-wells. After reading the

Declaration of Independence, Mr. Smith, at the point of total exhaustion, belted out:

"There's no compromise with truth. That's all I got up on this floor to say. When was it? A year ago, it seems like . . . Just get up off the ground, that's all I ask. Get up there with that lady that's up on top of this Capitol dome, that lady that stands for liberty. Take a look at this country through her eyes if you really want to see something. And you won't just see scenery; you'll see the whole parade of what Man's carved out for himself, after centuries of fighting. Fighting for something better than just jungle law, fighting so's he can stand on his own two feet, free and decent, like he was created, no matter what his race, color, or creed. That's what you'd see. There's no place out there for graft, or greed, or lies, or compromise with human liberties."

That was only in the movies. What would those streaming out of movie theaters in 1939, after watching *Mr. Smith Goes to Washington*, thought -- as Adolf Hitler was beginning to gobble up country after country in Europe – about a future American president, who believed Nazis are "fine people?"

The closest we had to a "Mr. Smith" moment was a rare rebuke of a sitting president from a Chief Justice of the U.S. Supreme Court. Chief Justice John Roberts, exasperated over Trump's criticism of a U.S. 9th Circuit appellate court judge for issuing a temporary restraining order blocking a Trump executive order on denying migrants crossing into the U.S. beyond ports of entry from seeking asylum, had stark words for Trump in a rare interview with the press. Roberts said, "We do not have Obama judges or Trump judges, Bush judges or Clinton judges. What we have is an extraordinary group of dedicated judges doing their level best to do equal right to those appearing before them. That independent judiciary is something we should all be thankful for."[11] Trump, in a tweet storm, fired back at Roberts his usual madman ramblings.

More troubling was Trump's bashing of the constitutionally-guaranteed independent press in the United States. Trump and his White House "sorcerer's apprentices" drew heavily from George Orwell's *1984*, the classic novel about a dystopian future of a pervasive "Big Brother," in crafting a policy of bashing the press as purveyors of "fake news." A dangerous form of "Newspeak," the official language of Big Brother's fictional super state of Oceania, crept into the American political lexicon.

Detention centers for children under the age of five -- youngsters who were forcibly separated from their parents at the U.S. southern border --

---

[11] Eli Watkins and Joan Biskupic, "Trump slams chief justice after Roberts chides the President," CNN, November 21, 2018.

were defined by the Trump administration as "tender age shelters." The term was coined by the Department of Homeland Security, which, itself, uses a title that is more reminiscent of the jargon of Nazi Germany and apartheid South Africa. Asylum-seeking immigrants to the United States became an "infestation," according to Trump and his creepy policy *gauleiter*, Stephen Miller. Infestation is the same word Adolf Hitler once used to describe Jews. Trump called for "merit-based immigration," but that was Trumpian Newspeak for white Europeans only. Trump publicly called for more Norwegian immigrants to the United States, rather than brown- or black-skinned people from elsewhere in the world.

In Trump's banana republic, lies became "alternative facts." Alternative facts were *de riguere* by senior Trump White House officials, including the chief disseminator of lies, White House counselor Kellyanne Conway. The "Bowling Green Massacre" was described by Conway as a terrorist attack ascribed to Muslims. The attack was pure fiction. It never occurred. Former Trump White House Press Secretary Sean Spicer similarly referred to a Muslim terrorist attack in Atlanta, also one that never occurred. In Trump's version of Oceania, alternative facts and alternate realities became the rule of the day.

Trump joined in the business of making up stories when he told a crowd in Florida in February 2017: "Look at what's happening last night in Sweden. Sweden, who would believe this. Sweden. They took in large numbers [of migrants]. They're having problems like they never thought possible." It turned out that nothing happened in

Sweden the previous night. Just more delusional crap from a delusional White House.

The press was clumped together by Trump officials as the "lying media," particularly when Trump's lies were called out in broadcasts and in print. "Fake news" was generally used by the White House to describe any information that ran counter to the propaganda constantly emanating from the Trump administration.

Trump called journalists "scum," "low-lifes," and "the lowest form of life." He called CNN's White House reporter Jim Acosta "crazy." In a Rose Garden news conference on October 1, 2018, Trump said to the press, "I consider you a part of the Democrat Party." By linking the press to the Democratic Party, Trump painted a bullseye on their backs.

Of course, the party has always been known as the Democratic Party. At one of Trump's cookie-cutter "rallies," held in West Virginia of September 29, 2018, Trump engaged in historical revisionism. He told the crowd, "The new platform of the Democrat Party—you notice I say Democrat Party? I hate the way it sounds, that's why I say it. Because it's really their name. It's not the Democratic Party."

It has been the Democratic Party since 1828. Originally, the party was known as the Democratic-Republican Party. The Democratic Party is the world's oldest continually active political party. However, Trump not only believed in his own alternate reality, but his own alternate history and his own alternate facts.

At his West Virginia hoedown, Trump continued his bizarre rant about the Democratic Party, "It flows nicer—the Democratic Party, but the real name is the Democrat Party . . . I hate the way it sounds and that's why I use it. But that's the real name. The Democrat Party. When you see Democratic Party, it's wrong. There's no name, Democratic Party."

Donald Trump's rants were no different than those of the Mad Hatter in Lewis Carroll's *Alice in Wonderland*. The following exchange could have been between Trump and one of his White House staff members:

Mad Hatter: "Why is a raven like a writing-desk?"
"Have you guessed the riddle yet?" the Hatter said, turning to Alice again.
"No, I give it up," Alice replied: "What's the answer?"
"I haven't the slightest idea," said the Hatter."

The Mad Hatter and Trump never had the slightest idea.

In psychiatry, Trump was known as a "delusional psychotic," an individual incapable of telling what is real from what is imagined. America could congratulate itself for elevating someone who was clinically insane to the presidency. Trump found himself in the company of some of the most insane leaders in the history of the world: King George III of England, King Charles VI of France, Emperor Justin II of Byzantium, King Ludwig II of Bavaria, Sultan Ibrahim I of the Ottoman Empire, Prince Sado of Korea, and Emperor Caligula of Rome.

There was also an element of Roman Emperor Claudius in Trump's decision-making process. Trump, like Claudius, entered politics later in life – although in Claudius's case, he became the co-consul to his brother, the tyrannical Caligula, at the age of 46. IN his late 60s, Trump entered U.S. presidential politics from the world of real estate, casinos, and entertainment. Claudius, like Trump, spent most of his pre-political life mired in games of chance and womanizing. Claudius had four wives, Trump three. Claudius, like Trump, was an avid fan of violent sports. Claudius liked Roman gladiator duels-to-the-death and chariot races, Trump preferred "professional" wrestling and boxing.

Trump, like Claudius, did not possess a keen intellect. However, both took on dangerous military adventures. Claudius invaded and annexed Britain in the 1st century AD. Although initially triumphant, Claudius's extension of Roman rule into the British Isles would eventually overextend the empire and lead to its collapse. Trump, although eschewing "regime change" conflicts encouraged by his two immediate predecessors – George W. Bush and Barack Obama – wholeheartedly embraced them after succumbing to the influence of neo-conservative policy advisers, like John Bolton.

Trump, as was the case with Claudius, suffered from neuro-psychiatric disorders that prompted him to constantly engage in socially inappropriate obsessions and compulsions.

Claudius eventually fell victim to the political designs of his fourth wife, Agrippina, who is believed to have engineered a plot to poison the emperor. Upon Claudius's death, Agrippina succeeded in having her son, Nero, placed on the throne. Claudius's demise is where the similarities to Trump generally ended. However, as seen in the summer of 2018, reports emerged of an attempt by some within the Trump administration to declare the old man mentally unfit for office and invoke the 25th Amendment to remove Trump from office.

Trump had no initial reaction when a deranged Maryland man, with a history of on-line support for Trump and a Maryland neo-Confederate leader, stormed the Annapolis offices of the *Capital-Gazette* newspaper and shot to death four journalists and one member of the staff. Trump wants his words to cause maximum harm and pain as do all sociopaths. One member of the newspaper staff told the author that he doubted that Ramos, who had a running eight-year long beef with the paper, would have resorted to mass murder had he not been triggered by Trump's dangerous and incendiary rhetoric.

Scientists and meteorologists working for the National Aeronautics and Space Administration (NASA) and the National Weather Service found themselves restricted from referring to "man-made climate change." Trump previously referred to the current global devastation being wrought by the man-made effects of rising temperatures and sea levels as a "Chinese hoax." Across the board, Trump and his cronies championed "junk science" studies, commissioned by Big Oil and Big Coal, over legitimate peer-reviewed academic research.

Before he was fired as administrator of the Environmental Protection Agency, Scott Pruitt ordered all references to "climate change" deleted from EPA web pages. "Climate change" was called the "double C-word" by Trump political hacks at the agency. The Trumpian "Newspeak" term was "weather extremes." Within Trump's EPA, "climate change" and "greenhouse gases" simply disappeared.

NEWSPEAK

Trump's Centers for Disease Control (CDC), America's premier public health agency and part of the Department of Health and Human Services, banned the use of seven words considered unacceptable. Modern-day Winston Smiths, professional language dissemblers working for Trump's very own Orwellian "Ministry of Truth" as language enforcers, prohibited the use of the words "diversity, entitlement, evidence-based, fetus, science-based, transgender and vulnerable." The Affordable Care Act was officially referred to as "Obamacare." "Sex education" became verboten. The term was changed to "sexual risk avoidance" through "abstention."

Education Secretary Betsy DeVos relied on the term "school choice" to mask her department's deep cuts to public education. DeVos's "school safety commission" specifically failed to mention the issue of guns and schools. DeVos was connected to the pyramid scheme-based

Amway Corporation through her husband, Richard DeVos, the son of the co-founder of the company and an heir to his father's fortune, and the infamous mercenary company Blackwater USA, through her brother, Erik Prince, the founder of the company.

Unsurprisingly, Betsy DeVos, who, according to former White House aide Omarosa, was called "Ditzy" DeVos by Trump, advocated guns in public schools to protect students and staff from threats like mass shooters and grizzly bears.[12] [13] The one thing Trump ever imparted that was true was that DeVos was, as he put it, "ditzy." One can hear Johnny Carson's lead in for a joke's punchline: "How dumb is Betsy DeVos? She's so dumb . . ."

DeVos was no friend of public education or public schools. She championed private schools and home schooling. Her confirmation as Education Secretary was so confidential,

---

[12] Tanya Wildt, "Omarosa says President Trump calls Betsy DeVos 'Ditzy DeVos,'" *USA Today*, August 14, 2018.

[13] Alastair Jamieson, "Betsy DeVos Cites Grizzly Bears During Guns-in-Schools Debate," NBC News, January 18, 2017.

Vice President Pence had to cast a tie-breaking vote in the Senate.

DeVos's opposition to public education resulted in ramifications around the country, particularly in states like Texas. In September 2018, the Texas State Board of Education, in act befitting Winston Smith in *1984*, voted to remove from social studies curriculum the following subjects: Hillary Clinton as the first major party female candidate for president, GOP conservative icon Barry Goldwater for just shits and giggles, revered inspiration for disabled people Helen Keller, What the Texas board did emphasize was teaching America's "Judeo-Christian values," even though there is nothing Christian about Israeli treatment of the Palestinians, who include many Christians. As one might expect, the following was inserted by the board into the history curriculum: "Arab rejection of the State of Israel has led to ongoing conflict." Moses replaced English political philosopher Thomas Hobbes as having influenced America's founding. Hobbes, who died in 1679, at least knew an "America" existed.[14]

Some Interior Department officials, as well as Ohio Representative and Dennis Hastert-like wrestling pervert Jim Jordan, agreed with Trump on his desire to change the name of Alaska's Denali mountain back to Mount

---

[14] Lauren McGaughy, "Texas board votes to eliminate Hillary Clinton, Helen Keller from history curriculum," *Dallas Morning News*, September 14, 2018.

McKinley. The aversion to the name Denali matches Trump's hostility to Native Americans and their sovereign tribal treaty rights.

Trump had also shown complete disdain for the sovereign rights of Native Americans. This was painfully apparent by his October 8, 2018 White House statement praising the "courage" of Christopher Columbus, who was responsible for ushering in an era that saw the genocide of 65 million indigenous peoples in the Western Hemisphere, from the Arctic Circle to Tierra del Fuego.

Trump's Federal Communications Commission, packed with telecommunications industry former lobbyists and executives, erroneously called "net neutrality," which has been abandoned, as "micro-management" of the Internet by the government. Nothing could be further from the truth as users began discovering by seeing constriction of bandwidth and the slowing down of Internet speed as AT&T, Verizon, and Comcast, which took over total control the FCC, hand over more bandwidth to operators like DirectTV and Netflix.

America's system of law enforcement and jurisprudence was called the "deep state" by Trump and his acolytes, many of whom, including Trump, have had a long history of being investigated by the Federal Bureau of Investigation, Department of Justice, and Securities and Exchange Commission for ties to organized crime syndicates. In another era, Trump would have found wholehearted support for calling the FBI "corrupt" from the likes of George "Baby Face" Nelson, Al Capone, Bugsy Siegel, Ma Barker, and George "Machine Gun" Kelly.

There was no longer any administration opposition to the menace of trusts and monopolies, recognized as inherently anti-business and anti-democratic since the days of President Theodore Roosevelt. Under Trump's "casino capitalism," the more monopolies the better, so long as those monopolies paid fealty to Trump's agenda.

And, speaking of casinos, Trump's long history with his Atlantic City and the mob – both the Italian and "Eurasian" variety – ensured that his administration was packed with individuals with dodgy backgrounds, including dalliances with the mafia. Not happy with the fact that, as Attorney General, Jeff Sessions's responsibilities did not entail acting as Trump's personal lawyer, the mobbed-up president wistfully demanded, "Where's my Roy Cohn?"[15] Cohen, the general counsel for Republican Senator Joseph McCarthy's "Red hunting" committee in the 1950s, later became Trump's personal lawyer. At the same time, Cohn was representing the bosses of the Genovese and Gambino crime families.

Under Trump, "immigrants" became known as "criminals." Neo-Nazis and Ku Klux Klansmen marching in Charlottesville, Virginia in support of the Confederacy and

---

[15] Michael Schmidt, "Obstruction Inquiry Shows Trump's Struggle to Keep Grip on Russia Investigation," *The New York Times*, January 4, 2018.

white supremacy became "fine people" in Trump's eyes. Within Jeff Sessions's Justice Department, the Anti-Trust and Civil Rights Divisions became very quiet places.

Ever fancying himself as the fictional Latin American dictator, Alfonse Simms (played by Richard Dreyfuss), in the comedy film, *Moon Over Parador*, Trump often referred to his administration as "my government," not seeming to recognize that the constitutional framework of the United States consists of three equal branches of government. Some "Banana Republicans" in Congress were willing to accept Trump's role as a Latin American *caudillo*. Trumpism was nothing more than caudillismo, repackaged and reformatted from Francisco Franco's Spain and Augusto Pinochet's Chile.

Donald Trump's collusion with Devin Nunes, the GOP chairman of the House Intelligence Committee, to derail the investigation of Justice Department Special Prosecutor Robert Mueller into the election malfeasance of the 2016 Trump campaign, was straight out of the script of the 1933 political thriller film, *Gabriel Over the White House*, which depicts a fictional U.S. president, Judson C. "Judd" Hammond (played by Walter Huston), assuming dictatorial powers with the connivance of some in Congress. Trump's packing of the Supreme Court with two right-wing ideologues, Neil Gorsuch and Brett Kavanaugh, were clear indications that Trump does not believe in constitution government, but a substitute unitary executive with him holding supreme power.

In the early 1980s, while attending the elite Jesuit-run male-only Georgetown Preparatory school in Washington,

DC, Gorsuch founded the "Fascism Forever Club." Gorsuch served as president of the club until his graduation in 1985. At the time he was attending the prep school, Gorsuch's mother, Anne Gorsuch, served as the administrator of the Environmental Protection Agency under Ronald Reagan.

In his graduation yearbook at Columbia University in 1988, Gorsuch's photograph is shown alongside his favorite quote, one made by Henry Kissinger on August 29, 1967: "The illegal we do immediately, the unconstitutional takes a little longer."

Of Trump's two selectees for the Supreme Court, one, Gorsuch, had a hankering for fascism at prep school and the other, Kavanaugh, had a problem with drinking and assaulting girls at the very same prep school during the same time frame. Later, Kavanaugh would champion the imperial and unitary presidency, beholden to none of the other co-equal branches of the federal government. Trump, in both appointments, was trying to stamp his imprimatur of fascism on the United States for decades into the future.

At a September 26, 2018 press conference in New York, Trump, in a pitiful attempt to defend Kavanaugh from multiple charges of sexual assault and misconduct at Georgetown Prep and at Yale University, invoked the first American president, George Washington. Trump charged that Washington had some accusations of sexual impropriety in his past. It was not the only time Trump showered disrespect upon a revered American president.

In one of America's lowest points in its history, Kavanaugh's defenders on the Senate Judiciary Committee, put themselves in the position of defending a federal judge accused of lying about sexual assault and alcohol abuse. It was a repeat of the 1991 Clarence Thomas nomination hearings, which featured a senile Strom Thurmond mistakenly hearing "Long John Silver," when the discussion was about Thomas's predilection for porn movies featuring a well-endowed actor with the stage name, "Long Dong Silver." And then there was Orrin Hatch, who also made a retirement appearance at the Kavanaugh hearing. In disputing Anita Hill's contention that Thomas sexually harassed her by asking about a pubic hair on a can of Coke, Hatch insisted that Hill's idea came from a passage from *The Exorcist* that referred to an "alien pubic hair" in a martini.

The author recalls being in a small town in south-central Pennsylvania during the Thomas hearings. One older gent, political persuasion unknown, commented at a local bar about what was transpiring during the hearings: "I've been to two county fairs, a goat fuckin' and a wagon-greasin' and I ain't ever seen anything so fucked up!" Thomas certainly primed the pump of American nitwittery to prepare us for Trump and Kavanaugh.

Kavanaugh's Judiciary Committee hearing was punctuated by its own references to delinquent behavior. In response to questions posed by Senator Sheldon Whitehouse (D-RI), Kavanaugh was evasive about the meaning of certain terms culled from his strangely "meticulous" calendars, in addition to his yearbook from his prep school days in the summer of 1982. Kavanaugh claimed that the term "boofing" referred to flatulence. In fact, the term had nothing to do with farting, the expulsion of gas from the rectum, but from the practice of ingesting illegal drugs through their insertion into rectum. A Supreme Court nominee who could not tell "intake" from "exhaust."

That prompted your author to concoct a special limerick for the occasion:

"There once was a jurist from Yale,
Who puked in many a pail.
He drank to excess,
And thought a 'No' was a 'Yes.'
And a boof was a fart from his tail."

There was the yearbook reference to "FFFFFFFourth of July," which did not mean a stuttering Georgetown Prep classmate who tried to say "Fuck You," which was stated by Kavanaugh, but the treatment of girls: "Find them, French them, Feel them, Finger them, Fuck them, Forget them." In answer to a question from Whitehouse about the meaning of "Devil's Triangle," Kavanaugh lied and said it was a "drinking game." In fact, it means the insertion of a penis into three orifices: mouth, vagina, and rectum.

Asked about the meaning of "ralphing," Kavanaugh replied that it was a reference to his vomiting after eating spicy food. Anyone who had a pulse in the 1960s onward and ever drank too much, knew that "going to see Ralph to buy a Buick" sounded like what someone belted out while puking into the toilet.

In the 1991 Thomas hearing, the role of the rotund Southern yokel was played by Senator Howell Heflin of Alabama. In 2018, that role was handled by Senator John Kennedy of Louisiana. Kennedy tried his best to emulate *Green Acres* character Eustace Charleston Haney, or just plain old "Mr. Haney," a con man played by comedian Pat Buttram.

Appearing on Fox News on October 2, 2018, Kennedy said of his Senate Democratic colleagues, "These are people — I'm not gonna name names — but I'm not sure they have a soul . . . I don't think their mother breastfed them. I think they went right to raw meat." That is what passed for GOP Senate material in 2018.

Listening to Kennedy ask Kavanaugh questions about belief in God and whether he was a good boy in prep school, reminded many of Buttram's squeaky and high-pitched Southern drawl and one uproarious joke Gene Autry's one-time sidekick told at a Friars Club roast of Rich Little in Beverly Hills in 1987.

Buttram said he had to fly out to Denver early the next morning. He explained that he was judging the annual sheep fucking contest just outside of Denver. Explaining why he was the judge, Buttram said, "last year's previous winner gets to be the judge this year." In 2018, Kavanaugh and Kennedy showed the world that they both could be judges at Colorado's annual sheep fucking contest.

The only thing missing from Louisiana Senator John Kennedy's biography is his failure to emulate Mr. Haney (Pat Buttram) and fly to Colorado to judge the annual "sheep fucking contest."

Trump's use of the presidency to threaten American citizens was also a low point in American political history. Using the comfortable façade of Twitter, Trump tweeted incessantly about firing and arresting people, acting like a tin-horn dictator of a banana republic.

In the 1964 film, *The Best Man*, which was based on a 1960 play written by Gore Vidal, two candidates are running for their party's presidential nomination. One is Senator Joe Cantwell, played by Cliff Robertson, a populist anti-Communist, who sees himself as the man of the people. The other is former Secretary of State William Russell, played by Henry Fonda.

Vidal revealed that Cantwell was based on Richard Nixon and Russell was an Adlai Stevenson-like principled intellectual. In the film, Cantwell says to Russell, "I don't understand you," whereupon Russell replies, "I know you don't. Because you have no sense of responsibility towards anyone or anything. And that is a tragedy in a man, and a disaster in a president." Not only was Vidal describing Nixon, but he was also foretelling Donald Trump.

Donald Trump: a pariah and a threat to world peace

In the area of foreign policy, Trump became an instant international pariah among America's allies and competitors.

Tossing away decades of surface-level evenhandedness on the Middle East, the Israeli illegally-occupied West Bank was referred to as "Judea and Samaria," by the Trump White House and its diplomatic surrogates. Judea and Samaria are the names assigned by the Israeli government to territory that was all-but-annexed by Israel. Other administration officials, including U.S. ambassador to the United Nations Nikki (Nimrata) Haley, referred to the Gaza Strip as "southern Israel." The official United Nations designation for the Palestinian territories is the "Occupied Palestinian Territory, East Jerusalem, and Gaza Strip." In May 2018, Trump moved the U.S. embassy from Tel Aviv to Jerusalem, thus conferring *de facto* U.S. recognition of Israel's illegal annexation of east Jerusalem.

Trump's decision to move the U.S. embassy had its roots with the religious politics of Jared Kushner, Trump's Middle East adviser and son-in-law. Kushner, a favorite of both Israeli Prime Minister Binyamin Netanyahu and pro-Netanyahu American casino tycoon Sheldon Adelson, tapped for his Middle East "envoy" team two rabidly pro-Israeli expansionist ideologues, U.S. ambassador to Israel David Friedman and "Special Representative for

International Negotiations" Jason Greenblatt. Friedman was an attorney with the law firm of Kasowitz, Benson, Torres & Friedman, which represented the Trump Organization. Greenblatt was the chief legal officer for the Trump Organization. Kushner, an Orthodox Jew, as was Friedman and Greenblatt, represented a far-right Zionist cabal that rejected both a Palestinian state and a single Israeli-Palestinian nation that fully enfranchised Palestinians as citizens of a secularized Israeli state. Kushner, Friedman, and Greenblatt favored an apartheid state, in which Palestinians remained second-class citizens.

In September 2018, being true to form, the White House announced that it was closing the Washington diplomatic mission of the Palestine Liberation Organization. The bearer of the bad news for the Palestinians was National Security Advisor John Bolton, whose first wife divorced him in the early 1980s for forcing her to participate, with him, in group sex trysts at a Manhattan swingers' club called Plato's Retreat. Yes, Bolton's personal tastes matched his degenerate foreign policy.[16]

---

[16] While an official in the Reagan administration's U.S. Agency for International Development (USAID), Bolton, according to divorce papers served by his ex-wife Christina Bolton, allegedly forced her to engage in orgies at Plato's Retreat. The Boltons were married in 1972 and they had no children. They separated on August 15, 1982, while Bolton was on a trip for USAID to Vienna, Austria. During the time Bolton frequented Plato's Retreat, the sex club was a popular haunt for Soviet KGB and Czechoslovak StB intelligence agents, who were on the lookout for blackmail information on Americans holding sensitive jobs. Interestingly, StB files from 1988 contained information about

Bolton's timing was very suspect. The closure came a few days before the September 13th anniversary of the signing of the Oslo Accords of 1993, the beginning of the Israeli-Palestinian peace dialogue.

Trump also cut off $251 million in assistance to the Palestinians, including $25 million that went to the East Jerusalem Hospital Network that funded cancer treatment for Palestinians.

To these developments, Israeli Prime Minister Binyamin Netanyahu could hardly contain his glee as Trump handed

---

one Donald Trump, a habitué of Studio 54, another problematic New York club -- a night spot known for drug use and underage prostitution.

A decade after his divorce, while an attorney for USAID contractor International Business & Technical Consultants Inc. (IBTCI), Bolton allegedly harassed Melody Townsel, a female sub-contractor for IBTCI, who had been working for USAID in Kyrgyzstan. What was very significant, in light of Bolton's selection as Trump's National Security Adviser, was Townsel's sub-contractor in Kyrgyzstan -- Black, Manafort, Stone & Kelly – the firm of Trump's convicted presidential campaign manager Paul Manafort and Roger Stone, the infamous GOP dirty trickster. According to Townsel, Bolton made her life miserable during their time together in Russia.

him and his right-wing government every U.S. bargaining chip held in reserve for some five decades.

Trump's plans to bring about a Middle East peace deal was a lot of hogwash from the very outset of his administration. Rather than choose as his intermediaries those who had even the slightest degree of impartiality, Trump selected as his "troika" of negotiators, three of the most insanely pro-Netanyahu characters he could dredge up: his son-in-law Jared Kushner, senior adviser to the president and special envoy for Middle East peace negotiations; former executive vice president and chief legal officer of the Trump Organization Jason Greenblatt, assistant to the president and Special Representative for International Negotiations; and David Friedman, Trump's former bankruptcy lawyer with the firm Kasowitz, Benson, Torres & Friedman, as U.S. ambassador to Israel. One would be hard-pressed to tell the difference between a Trump Middle East peace negotiation strategy session and a Mah-Jongg tournament in Miami Beach.

Trump proceeded to rapidly carry out numerous Israeli wishes, including de-certification of the P5+1 (China, France, Russia, the United Kingdom, and the United States; plus Germany) Joint Comprehensive Plan of Action (JCPOA) with Iran over its nuclear power program, supporting Saudi actions against Qatar and Yemen, and cutting off direct U.S. aid to the Palestinian Authority and to the United Nations Relief and Works Agency (UNWRA), which assists Palestinian refugees. Trump continued to support Israeli-backed jihadist rebel groups battling Syrian President Bashar al Assad, supported pro-Israeli Egyptian President Abdel Fattah al-Sisi's economic blockade of the

Hamas government of Gaza, and froze security assistance to Pakistan.

The White House also relied on a discredited and arcane report from Israeli Prime Minister Binyamin Netanyahu that suggests Iran had a nuclear weapons program. Piggybacking on the ludicrous allegation by Netanyahu, which was designed to convince Trump to withdraw from the six-power nuclear agreement with Iran, White House Press Secretary Sarah Huckabee Sanders said Netanyahu's "facts are consistent with what the United States has long known: Iran has a robust, clandestine nuclear weapons program that it has tried and failed to hide from the world and from its own people." The White House later changed "has" to "had."

The phoniness of Israel's allegations about Iran hearkened back to George W. Bush's allegation that Saddam Hussein acquired yellow cake uranium from Niger. The basis for that charge was a forged Niger government document provided by neocon agents-of-influence, linked to Israeli intelligence, that were based in Washington and Rome.

According to Bob Woodward's tell-all book about the Trump administration, *Fear: Trump in the White House,* Trump ordered Secretary of Defense James Mattis to assassinate Assad, which would have been a clear violation of U.S. law. Trump ordered Mattis: Let's fucking kill him! Let's go in. Kill the fucking lot of them," referencing Assad and his government. Mattis, according to Woodward, responded that he "would get right on it," then telling an assistant, "We're not going to do any of that. We're going to be much more measured." Mattis also described Trump as possessing the understanding of a "fifth or sixth grader."[17]

The governments of Venezuela, Iran, and Syria were called "regimes" by Trump foreign policy officials. "Regime change" was the stated goal of the Trump State Department regarding all three countries. After Trump's disastrous and unproductive June 12, 2018 summit in Singapore with North Korean leader Kim Jong Un, some sectors of the Trump administration continued to refer to the North Korean government as a "regime," while Secretary of State Mike Pompeo elevated the terminology to "DPRK," or Democratic People's Republic of Korea."

Speaking to the UN General Assembly on September 25, 2018, Trump canned the "Rocket Man" pejorative in favor of "Chairman Kim" to describe the North Korean leader. It did not matter much to the other world leaders and diplomats gathered in New York for the annual plenary meeting of the General Assembly.

Trump led off his speech, which was full of invective against the post-World War II United Nations-led system of peacekeeping and international oversight, to boast about his accomplishments as president of the United States.

In a speech widely attributed to his two fascist-minded advisers, John Bolton and Stephen Miller, Trump said, "In less than two years, my administration has accomplished more than almost any administration in the history of our

---

[17] Bob Woodward, *Fear: Trump in the White House*, (New York: Simon & Schuster, 2018).

country." Trump's pretentious crowing resulted in mild laughter from the assembly hall. Trump replied to the laughter, "Didn't expect that reaction, but that's okay." That resulted in an outbreak of louder laughter from the leaders and delegates. Trump was the laughing stock of the world and it came at the expense of every American who believed they still retained an iota of dignity in the eyes of the world.

In the foreign policy portion of his speech, Trump warned that Germany would be totally dependent on Russian energy exports, a statement that elicited laughter from the German delegation. Trump also invoked the arcane Monroe Doctrine of 1823. Trump said, "It has been the formal policy of our country since President Monroe that we reject the interference of foreign nations in this hemisphere and in our own affairs." It was a clear threat to Venezuela and Cuba, which Trump singled out for promoting "socialism." It was as if the UN had been taken back in time to the heated anti-Communist jargon of the 1950s.

Russia and China, which had been developing closer ties with Latin America and the Caribbean, were the chief targets of Trump's threat to enforce the Monroe Doctrine. However, Latin American nations had always bristled at any suggestion that the "gringo empire" of the north might revert to "gunboat diplomacy" and installation of "banana republics" subservient to Washington throughout the western hemisphere.

In August 2017, while standing next to Secretary of State Tillerson at his Bedminster, New Jersey golf resort, Trump mused about invading Venezuela. Trump said, with an irritated Tillerson looking on, "We have many options for Venezuela, this is our neighbor . . . We're all over the world and we have troops all over the world in places that are very, very far away, Venezuela is not very far away and the people are suffering and dying. We have many options for Venezuela including a possible military option if necessary." Venezuelan President Maduro had tried to place a phone call to Trump. It was refused. Venezuelan Defense Minister Vladimir Padrino called Trump's threat of a military invasion an "act of craziness" and "supreme extremism."[18]

Trump continued to harbor a desire for an invasion of Venezuela, pressing Colombian President Juan Manuel Santos and a dinner meeting with pro-U.S. Latin American leaders on the sideline of the 2017 UN General Assembly meeting in September 2017.[19]

Trump also warned the gathered world leaders that U.S. foreign aid would only go to countries that cozied up to Trump and his fragile ego. Trump said, "We are taking a hard look at US foreign assistance. Moving forward, we are only going to give foreign aid to those who respect us and frankly are our friends."

---

[18] Julian Borger, "Trump repeatedly suggested Venezuela invasion, stunning top aides – report, *The Guardian*, July 5, 2018.

[19] *Ibid.*

Trump also lashed out at the International Criminal Court, the JCPOA with Iran, the Organization of Petroleum Exporting Countries (OPEC), the UN Human Rights Council, the Global Compact on Migration, and, without mentioning them, but hinting at U.S. disapproval of their very existence, the World Trade Organization, the UN High Commission for Refugees, and the UN Relief and Works Agency for Palestine Refugees in the Near East (UNRWA).

Trump singled out for condemnation the government of Iran, which he erroneously called the "world's leading sponsor of terrorism,"[20] the government of President Bashar al-Assad in Syria, and the government of President Nicolas Maduro of Venezuela. Trump lauded some of the world's worst human rights violators, including Israel, Poland, India, and Saudi Arabia.

Prior to Trump's "bromance" with Kim, their relationship was befitting that of a cobra and mongoose. The North Korean government engaged in a bitter war of words with Trump after the U.S. commander-in-chief resorted to calling Kim "rocket man" in tweets and before the United Nations General Assembly, normally the domain of tactful diplomats. Trump's juvenile name-calling resulted in North Korea referring to Trump as a "dotard," an arcane English word meaning a feeble and senile old man.

---

[20] The accusation that Iran was the "world's leading sponsor of terrorism" was quintessential propaganda regularly employed by Israel, the anti-Iranian government terrorist group/cult Mojahedin-e-Khalq (MEK), and neo-conservative think tanks funded by Zionist groups in the United States.

North Korea, viewing Trump's renunciation of the Joint Comprehensive Plan of Action (JCPOA) nuclear weapons agreement with Iran, had no desire to reach a nuclear deal with Washington after witnessing America's signature of any agreement or treaty as not worth the paper it's printed on.

When it came to which leader was crazier – Trump or Kim – let the historical record state that North Korea signed the Paris Climate Accord, an agreement Trump renounced and denounced.

Prior to the withdrawal of the United States from the United Nations Human Rights Council, the State Department objected to documents calling out governments for "racism" and "xenophobia."

In Trump's world, neither racism nor xenophobia were considered dangerous, but were fully embraced as public policy. To Trump, African countries and Haiti were "shit holes" and Nigerians were living in "huts." Trump and his policymakers continued to use the loaded right-wing term, "radical Islamic terrorism," when most Islamic religious leaders of the Sunni, Shi'a, Sufi, and other Islamic sects reject terrorism. The Central Intelligence Agency's "Factbook" erroneously listed Al Qaeda as being aligned with Iran, even though Al Qaeda was born from Saudi Arabian Wahhabism and is considered a mortal enemy by predominantly Shi'a Iran.

Trump summed up his overall ignorance about Africa at a luncheon held on the sidelines of the plenary meeting of the United Nations General Assembly in New York on September 20, 2017. Trump told the presidents of Côte d'Ivoire, Ethiopia, Ghana, Guinea, Namibia, Nigeria, Senegal, South Africa, and Uganda, "I have so many friends going to your countries trying to get rich."

Trump also referred to the health care system of "Nambia," a non-existent country believed to be Namibia. If only Mutual of Omaha's Wild Kingdom host, Marlin Perkins, was still alive. Someone who could, at least, provide rudimentary geography lessons to the American president.

On June 9, 2018, Trump managed to invent another African country in a tweet: "My thoughts and prayers are with the families of our serviceman who was killed and his fellow servicemen who were wounded in Somolia [sic]. They are truly all HEROES."

Trump could probably be convinced that Somolia borders on Wakanda, the fictional home country of the superhero Black Panther.

On August 22, 2018, Trump tweeted about a false report he saw on Fox News. Trump mistakenly believed that there was large-scale killing of white farmers in South Africa. Trump tweeted: "I have asked Secretary of State @SecPompeo to closely study the South Africa land and farm seizures and expropriations and the large scale killing of farmers. South African Government is now seizing land from white farmers." In fact, murders of both blacks and whites on South African farms were at their lowest in 19 years. But facts mattered little to either Fox or Trump.

The South African government immediately protested Trump's inane tweet to the U.S. embassy in Pretoria. The government rejected Trump's "false information" and rejected what it called "this narrow perception which only seeks to divide our nation and reminds us of our colonial past."[21]

How did Trump react to his diplomatic mugging of South Africa? He nominated as U.S. ambassador to the country, a South African-born handbag designer from Palm Beach, Lana Marks. Her handbags retailed from between $10,000 and $400,000. Like Trump, Marks had a problem with telling the truth. She claimed to have played professional tennis in Wimbledon and the South African and French Open tournaments. However, according to veterans of the tournaments and official records, no one named Lana

---

[21] Robbie Gramer and Colum Lynch, "In Tacit Rebuke, U.S. Embassy in South Africa Rejects Trump Tweet," *Foreign Policy*, August 29, 2018.

Marks or Lana Banks (her maiden name) ever having been a professional international tennis player.[22]

Marks did represent Bermuda in the Maccabi Games in Israel in 1985. However, after she and her husband were found to have violated Bermuda's immigration laws, they were expelled from the island.[23] Donald Trump reveled in appointing such grifters, many members of the Mar-a-Lago club in Palm Beach, to represent the United States and ambassadors abroad.

Trump continued to show his utter ignorance about Africa when he told visiting Spanish King Felipe and Queen Letizia, who were accompanied to the White House by Spanish Foreign Minister Josep Borell, that Spain should solve the African migrant problem by building a wall across the Sahara.[24] Aside from two small Spanish enclaves on the Mediterranean coast of North Africa – Ceuta and Melilla – Spain does not control any other territory in Africa. To the people of Spain and Africa, Trump demonstrated, once again, that he was an ignorant fool.

---

[22] Jason Burke and Sabrina Siddiqui, "Trump reportedly picks handbag designer as ambassador to South Africa," *The Guardian*, October 2, 2018.

[23] Michael Bleby, "We spoke to handbag designer and soon-to-be US ambassador to SA: this is what she said," *Business Day*, October 1, 2018.

[24] Sam Jones, "Donald Trump urged Spain to 'build the wall' – across the Sahara," *The Guardian*, September 19, 2018.

In what certainly could been of further interest to Justice Department Special Counsel Robert Mueller, Trump's admission that his "friends" go to Africa to "get rich," provided further insight into the international criminal syndicate that illegally supported Trump's political campaign.

Among Trump "friends" getting rich in Africa are expatriate billionaire oligarchs living in Israel, Britain, and other countries who are viciously exploiting Africa's natural resources, including diamonds, gold, platinum, oil, and rare earth minerals. Some of these brigands who are robbing Africa blind are business associates of Trump son-in-law Jared Kushner and his family.

Trump saw Africa as one huge "get rich quick scheme." That rhetoric came as music to the ears of the African grifters -- presidents like Uganda's Yoweri Museveni, Zuma, and Côte d'Ivoire's Alassane Ouattara -- who were present at the luncheon and who have also made certain that their offshore bank accounts are flush with bribe money paid by Trump's rich pals.

Although one could understand an out-and-out racist like Trump calling African nations and Haiti shitholes, it is bananas how he treated Montenegro's prime minister, Dusko Markovic, at the North Atlantic Treaty Organization summit in Brussels on May 26, 2017. During a photo op in Brussels, Trump infamously shoved Markovic out of the way so that he could stand in front of the other NATO leaders for cameras. Just two weeks prior to Montenegro becoming a NATO member, Trump's insult resulted in several Montenegrin politicians of all stripes demanding that sanctions be imposed against the United States for "humiliating" Markovic.

A week after Trump attended another NATO summit in Brussels in May 2018, he took aim, once again, at Montenegro. In an interview on May 16, 2018 with Fox News's bowtie-wearing propagandist Tucker Carlson -- whose father, Dick Carlson, once led Ronald Reagan's propaganda efforts at the Voice of America -- Trump said, "Montenegrins are very aggressive people," adding, "they may get aggressive and congratulations, you're in World War III . . . It's very unfair because they aren't even paying and we are protecting them."[25]

Trump would later involve the President of Finland, Sauli Niinisto, in his fantasy world of lies and sociopathy. While visiting California to witness the aftermath of deadly and destructive forest fires, Trump falsely recounted a conversation with Niinisto during the World War I armistice centenary observances in Paris. Trump, in a bald-faced lie, said Niinisto told him that Finns spent "a lot of time on raking and cleaning" their forest floors tp prevent wildfires. Trump said, "I was with the president of Finland, and he said: 'We have a much different . . . we're a forest nation.' And they spent a lot of time on raking and

---

[25] "Very aggressive': Trump suggests Montenegro could cause world war three," *The Guardian*, July 19, 2018.

cleaning and doing things, and they don't have any problem."[26]

Niinisto said he never told Trump and such thing and Trump's lie became the source of derision and laughter throughout Finland. Not only was Trump, once again, the butt of a joke, America was the laughing stock of the entire world.

Trump appeared anxious to start wars. In March 2017, he tweeted, "trade wars are good, and easy to win." To the contrary, trade wars have often led to shooting wars.

After his reference to African nations, Haiti, Honduras, and El Salvador as shitholes, the African Union relayed its "shock, dismay and outrage" over the comments. Botswana called in the U.S. ambassador in Gaborone and demanded an explanation of Trump's remarks. In the past, Trump referred to South Africa as a "mess." Trump's overt racism and misogyny was on full display in how he described any government led by a person of color, whether it was South Africa, or London under Mayor Sadiq Khan (who Trump called "pathetic"), San Juan, Puerto Rico under Mayor Carmen Yulin Cruz, Oakland under Mayor Libby Schaaf, or Flint under Mayor Karen Weaver. New York Mayor Bill DiBlasio, whose wife is African-American, also came in for Trump's personal insults.

---

[26] "California wildfires: Finland bemused by Trump raking comment," BBC, November 19, 2018.

After Trump disinvited the Super Bowl winning Philadelphia Eagles to the White House, Philadelphia Mayor Jim Kenney summed up what many mayors across the United States thought. Kenney called Trump a "tyrant" who was "trying to turn this country into a dictatorship."[27]

Trump repeated his snub of professional athletes when he disinvited from a White House visit, the 2018 National Basketball Association champions, the Golden State Warriors. Some members of the 2018 National Hockey League champions, the Washington Capitals, said they would take a pass on a visit to the White House.

Trump's snubbing of the professional athletes of three major sports and his call for a boycott of motorcycle giants, Harley-Davidson and Indian Motorcycles, is about what one might expect from an anti-democratic fascist placed in the Oval Office by a non-American interest.

At a White House immigration meeting, Trump said of Haitian asylum grantees in the United States, "Why do we need more Haitians? Take them out." He also said Haitians all have Aids" and Nigerians living in the United States "never to back to their mud huts."[28] Never in the history of

---

[27] Alex Sundby, "Philadelphia mayor calls Trump a "tyrant" after White House snubs Eagles," CBS News, June 4, 2018.

[28] Michael D. Shear and Julie Hirschfeld Davis, "Stoking Fears, Trump Defied Bureaucracy to Advance Immigration Agenda," *The New York Times*, December 23, 2017.

the American republic had such an ignorant buffoon sat behind the presidential desk.

In Trump's world, small and poor nations are aggressive and a threat to him. This guy is so bananas that he probably believes that Liechtenstein, San Marino, Andorra, Tuvalu, Niue, and eSwatini pose military threats to the United States. Trump probably believes the 1959 Cold War spoof film, *The Mouse That Roared*, starring Peter Sellers and was based on the 1955 novel of the same title, was a documentary. In the film, the fictional Grand Duchy of Fenwick kidnaps the inventor of the devastating Q-bomb after the Grand Fenwick Expeditionary Force, armed only with long bows, invades New York City during a nuclear attack drill.

To Trump, appointing cronies to ambassadorial posts was not an exception, but a rule. The posts of U.S. ambassador to Germany and Estonia, as well as the Assistant Secretary of State for Near Eastern Affairs, saw Trump nominate neo-conservative candidates with sordid histories. Out of the three, one was unsuccessful. Trump's nominee to be ambassador to Estonia was withdrawn after the Estonian government complained that the individual due to take up the post in Tallinn was unacceptable to them.

The first bad actor was Richard Grenell, the gay former man servant, or "coffee boy" --to use a Trump term -- of John Bolton, while "Mr. Walrus" served as the unconfirmed U.S. ambassador to the United Nations in the

George W. Bush administration. Grenell was confirmed by the U.S. Senate to be U.S. ambassador to Germany on April 26, 2018 in a 56-42 vote.

Grenell, like Trump, became a notorious Twitter troll. After Trump withdrew from the Iran nuclear accord, Grenell tweeted from his post in Berlin, "German companies doing business in Iran should wind down operations immediately." An apt response by the Germans would have been the comment Trump's indicted personal lawyer, Michael Cohen, gave in response to a remark on CNN: "Says who?"

David Satterfield was called out of Foreign Service retirement to become the acting Assistant Secretary of State for Near Eastern Affairs. While previously serving in various State Department roles, Satterfield helped oversee the unraveling of the nation-states of Iraq, Syria, and Libya. In 2008, *The New York Times* identified Satterfield as an unindicted co-conspirator in the Justice Department's espionage case against American Israel Public Affairs Committee (AIPAC) officials Steve Rosen and Keith Weissman and Department of Defense official Lawrence Franklin. Satterfield was identified as "USGO-2" (U.S. Government employee number 2) in the indictment of Rosen, Weismann, and Franklin.[29] At the time, Satterfield, a former U.S. ambassador to Lebanon, was serving as

---

[29] David Johnston and James Risen, "U.S. Diplomat Is Named In Secrets Case," *The New York Times*, August 18, 2005.

Deputy Chief of Mission in Baghdad under U.S. ambassador Zalmay Khalilzad. Yes, that Khalilzad, the one who was negotiating with the Taliban in Afghanistan about a UNOCAL pipeline through the country prior to 9/11 and while the Taliban was hosting a guy named Osama Bin Laden in a cave in Afghanistan.

While serving at the State Department, Satterfield defended security contracts awarded to such private mercenary companies as Blackwater, Triple Canopy, and Dyncorp. Blackwater founder Erik Prince's sister, Betsy DeVos, served as Education Secretary in the Trump Cabinet. Prince came under investigation by Special Counsel Mueller for colluding with foreign countries on behalf of the Trump 2016 presidential campaign.

It was more than apparent that with Trump's presidency, Prince had a green light to engage in as much skullduggery and chicanery as any mercenary might desire. From his base of operations in Abu Dhabi, where he maintained the headquarters for his post-Blackwater mercenary firm, Reflex Responses (R2), Prince became involved in secret military operations in Yemen, South Sudan, Somalia, Mali, Niger, Burkina Faso, and Libya. Prince, who used code names like "Echo Papa" and "EP," was a ubiquitous visitor to arms manufacturers and other defense firms throughout Europe, the Middle East, and Asia.[30]

Prince owned significant shares in Airborne Technologies, an aviation company based in Wiener Neustadt, Austria, just outside of Vienna. Prince and his colleagues use a

---

[30] Jeremy Scahill and Matthew Cole, "Echo Papa Exposed," *The Intercept*, April 11, 2016.

shady Bulgarian company, LASA Engineering Ltd., to modify the Thrush 510G fixed-wing aircraft, designed as a crop duster, with machine guns, bullet-resistant components, forward-looking infrared (FLIR) cameras, and lasers used for precision weapons targeting. The export of crop dusters-turned-warplanes by Prince represents a clear violation of the intent and spirit of the U.S. International Traffic in Arms and Export Administration Regulations (ITAR/EAR). San Marino, a republic nestled within Italy, discovered that Prince was registering his militarized crop dusters in that nation. It proceeded to cancel at least one aircraft registration.[31]

In a case of life imitating art, THRUSH was the name of the international criminal network battled by UNCLE's Napoleon Solo (Robert Vaughn) and Illya Kuryakin (David McCallum) in the *Man from UNCLE* television series.

In a tweet sent on January 1, 2018, Trump destroyed years invested in the U.S.-Pakistani security relationship. He wrote: "The United States has foolishly given Pakistan more than 33 billion dollars in aid over the last 15 years, and they have given us nothing but lies & deceit, thinking of our leaders as fools. They give safe haven to the terrorists we hunt in Afghanistan, with little help. No more!"

Pakistan's Foreign Minister Khawaja Asif responded to Trump's Twitter tantrum by declaring in a tweet that, "He [Trump] has tweeted against us [Pakistan] and Iran for his

---

[31] *Ibid*.

domestic consumption." Possibly true, with the caveat that most Trump supporters could not find either Pakistan or Iran on a map.

Trump's nominee to be U.S. ambassador to Estonia, retired U.S. Naval Reserve Rear Admiral Edward "Sonny" Masso, did not fare as well as Grenell and Satterfield. Masso was nominated by Trump in September 2017. On May 24, 2018, Masso's nomination was withdrawn after the Estonian government complained about the nomination. Masso served with Steve Bannon on the *USS Paul F. Foster* (DD-964). The two became lifelong friends. Masso briefly served as chief operating officer of the North Carolina Department of Public Safety from February to August 2013. He, along with his boss, Secretary of Public Safety Kieran Shanahan, abruptly resigned their posts without giving a reason. Raleigh, the state capital, was rife with rumors of a scandal involving the twin resignations.[32]

Additionally, Masso worked for defense contractors Anteon Corporation and SAIC during his stints in Washington, DC; founded a consulting firm, Flagship Corporation; served on the board of advisers of the Jewish Institute of National Security Affairs (JINSA), an organization whose motto is "Securing America, Strengthening Israel"; and wrote for Breitbart News, where his pal, Bannon, had been the editor.

Trump appointed as ambassadors some of his billionaire cronies who were members of his Mar-A-Lago club in Florida. GOP donor Robin Bernstein received the

---

[32] Thomas Mills, "From Shenanigans to Scandal?" Politics North Carolina <politicsnc.com>, July 28, 2013.

ambassadorship to the Dominican Republic, where the Trump Organization has business interests. Her only qualification appeared to be her frequent attendance at swank parties in Palm Beach, the Hamptons, and Washington, DC. Mar-a-Lago member and financier Duke Buchan III was nominated to be ambassador to Spain.

Woody Johnson, the owner of the New York Jets football team received the much-coveted ambassadorship to the Court of St. James in London.

Thankfully, some of Trump's ambassadorial nominees failed to see confirmation by the Senate. One was Diana Ecclestone, wife of Trump's fellow Palm Beach mansion dweller, real estate tycoon E. Llwyd Ecclestone, Jr. In July 2018, Llwyd Eccelstone's youngest daughter, Wendy Walker Mendelsohn, sued her father, claiming that he molested her when she was ten years old and that he took no action against her older brother, six years her senior, for molesting her over a two-year period. Ecclestone denied the charges.[33]

After Ms. Ecclestone's ambassadorship to Barbados failed to materialize, in February 2018, Trump nominated another problematic billionaire to be the ambassador to Barbados. He was Leandro Rizzuto, Jr., a member of Mar-a-Lago and a senior executive of Conair. Rizzuto was also a major Trump fundraiser. Rizzuto also spread various

---

[33] Alexandra Clough, "Ecclestone daughter accuses powerful developer of child sex abuse," Palm Beach Post, July 3, 2018.

conspiracy theories via Twitter. His nomination, which also would have accredited him to Saint Kitts and Nevis, Saint Lucia, Antigua and Barbuda, the Commonwealth of Dominica, Grenada, and Saint Vincent and the Grenadines, ran into trouble in the Senate.

Trump's ambassador to Italy was Lewis Eisenberg, a New York financier, who was Chairman of the Port Authority of New York and New Jersey during the 9/11 attack. He was also a past chairman of the finance committee of the Republican National Committee. Trump sent to Poland Georgette Mosbacher, a cosmetic firm owner and frequent contributor on Fox News.

Trump's ambassador to New Zealand and Samoa was former Senator Scott Brown (R-MA). When Brown arrived in Samoa to present his credentials to the head of state, he was accused of acting in an inappropriate manner with female food servers and U.S. Peace Corps volunteers. The State Department quickly covered up the incident. State's Inspector-General only stated it "conducted an independent review of the allegations and reported its findings to the department," adding that Brown was "counseled on standards of conduct for government employees."[34]

---

[34] Joshua Miller, "Scott Brown's pay is $155,000 per year. The benefits are priceless," *The Boston Globe*, November 18, 2017.

Trump could not have a better ambassador than Brown, a person who strove to emulate the boorish behavior of the president.

It was not merely nations having troubled relations with the United States that were subjected to Trump's boorish and adolescent insults, but longtime allies and friends of the United States.

During a July 2018 visit to the United Kingdom, Trump, in a meeting with Queen Elizabeth II at Windsor Castle, decided to cut in front of the British monarch, an uncouth breach of protocol. Trump also tweeted, while departing England for Scotland, that he "leaving the U.K." The U.K., for the time being, is composed of four countries, England, Scotland, Wales, and Northern Ireland. It is something every child has been taught in public schools in America. Apparently, Trump, who decided "Ditzy DeVos" should be his Education Secretary, places very little importance in learning the basics of geography and history.

During the 2016 campaign, Trump insulted Belgium by calling Brussels a "hellhole," but adding, "Belgium is a beautiful city."

At a September 26, 2018 news conference at the United Nations, Trump acknowledging a question from Rahim Rashidi of Kurdistan TV, said, "Yes, please, Mr. Kurd. Go ahead." There was no rational explanation for Trump from his senior staff. He was simply ignorant and a complete asshole and that sort of crass combination belonged nowhere near the United Nations.

It seemed that everywhere Trump visited, he left a trail of those who were insulted, hustled, and disgusted by his boorish and childish behavior.

Since the dark advent of the Trump administration, the number of foreign officials facing U.S. travel bans and asset freezes also skyrocketed.

Banned from U.S. travel and a U.S. asset freeze were Venezuelan Vice President Tareck El Aissami and *Petroleos de Venezuela SA* (PDVSA) Chief Financial Officer Simon Zerpa Delgado. The U.S. assets of Venezuelan President Nicolas Maduro were frozen in July 2017. Others Latin Americans similarly sanctioned included General Commissioner Francisco "Paco" Diaz of the Nicaraguan National Police; Fidel Moreno, secretary at Managua City Hall and Sandinista party secretary; and Francisco "Chico" Lopez, treasurer of ruling Sandinista National Liberation Front party.

U.S. asset freezing orders were also ordered on Turkey's Interior Minister Suleyman Soylu and Justice Minister Abdulhamit Gul. The Trump administration also threatened to freeze the assets of Cambodian President Hun Sen.

In August 2018, Trump signed the Zimbabwe Democracy and Economic Recovery Amendment Act of 2018, also called ZIDERA, which continued to apply U.S. visa bans and asset freezes on Zimbabwe President Emmerson Mnangagwa and officials of his government. In May 2017, the Trump administration refused to grant U.S. visas to delegates hoping to attend the annual African Global and Economic Development Summit in California.

U.S. asset freezes were being contemplated on Prime Minister Haider al-Abadi, former Iraqi prime minister Nouri al-Maliki, former Iraqi minister of finance Hoshyar Zebari, Mohamed al-Karbouli, Ahmed Nouri al-Maliki, and Hassan al-Anbari merely because they maintained friendly ties with Iran. The Trump administration also threatened to impose visa bans and asset freezes on top Maldives officials, including President Yameen Abdul Gayoom.

Trump's visa ban and asset freeze frenzy were also applied to South Sudan's defense minister, Kuol Manyang Juk, as well as government minister Martin Elia Lomuro and information minister Michael Makuei.

These actions were in addition to bans previously imposed on government officials and citizens of Iran, Libya, North Korea, Somalia, Syria, Laos, Guinea, Eritrea, Ghana, Gambia, Chad, and Yemen.

The Trump administration threatened visa bans and asset freezes on Chinese government officials for alleged mistreatment of Muslim Uighurs in the western Xinjiang province. Those subject to possible sanctions included Chinese diplomat Hu Lianhe, Chen Quanguo, Communist Party chief in Xinjiang and member of the Politburo of the Chinese Communist Party; Xinjiang Deputy Communist Party Secretary Shohret Zakir; and Xinjiang Politics and Law Commission chairman Zhu Hailun.

In a September 26, 2018 speech, while acting in his capacity as the UN Security Council's rotating president, Trump told the gathered world leaders and diplomats that China was behind a plot to "meddle" in America's 2018 mid-term election because they were upset with tariffs imposed by his administration. As "proof" Trump pointed to China's public relations advertisement insert buys in farm belt newspapers, including *The Des Moines Register*. Although such paid inserts are common practice by foreign embassies and travel agencies, Trump saw some sinister conspiracy being afoot. During a press conference Trump held in New York later that day, he said, "The President of China has very very much respect for my very very large brain."

During speeches at three separate UN events, a session on international narcotics trafficking, the General Assembly, and the Security Council meeting, Trump demonstrated to the entire world that he was nothing more than a senile pant load of incontinency . . . and inconsistency.

In December 2017, the Trump administration applied similar sanctions on the Commander-in-Chief of the Myanmar armed forces, Senior General Min Aung Hlaing; Major General Maung Maung Soe; Major General Khin Maung Soe; and other top Myanmar military officers.

The United States claimed its sanctions against China, Zimbabwe, Venezuela, Nicaragua, and Myanmar were in the interest of "human rights," even as the Trump administration continued to detain children separated from their asylum-seeking parents at the U.S.-Mexican border, earning the condemnation of the United Nations and countries around the world.

Some leaders and diplomats of foreign nations were even detained or arrested when they arrive in New York to attend UN sessions.

In June 2017, the North Korean government lodged a protest with the United Nations over the detention of its diplomats who were departing New York at John F. Kennedy airport in New York. The North Koreans said that accused Department of Homeland Security officers and JFK airport police seized a diplomatic package, which carried a valid diplomatic courier certificate. The U.S. action violated the 1961 Vienna Convention and U.S.-U.N. Treaty of 1947.

Such harassment began, in earnest, just a few weeks after Trump was inaugurated as president. In February 2017, former Norwegian Prime Minister Kjell Magne Bondevik was caught up in Trump's visa ban against visitors from Muslim nations. Bondevik was detained at Dulles International Airport outside of Washington and subjected to questioning about an Iranian visa in his diplomatic passport.[35]

In June 2018, America's Israeli-style harassment was also meted out to former Spanish Foreign Minister and NATO Secretary General Javier Solana. He was denied a U.S. visa waiver because he had visited Iran in 2013 to attend President Hassan Rouhani's inauguration. Solana told the Spanish Antena-3 television, "It's a bit of a mean decision .

---

[35] Nadia Khomami, "Former Norway PM held at Washington airport over 2014 visit to Iran," *The Guardian*, February 3, 2017.

. . I don't think it's good because some people have to visit these complicated countries to keep negotiations alive."[36]

Even past U.S. foreign policy chiefs were not spared Trump's vicious response to anyone attempting diplomatic dialogue with Iran. Former Secretary of State John Kerry was singled out for potential prosecution under a so-called violation of the arcane and Logan Act of 1799. Kerry had met with Iranian Foreign Minister Javad Zarif "three or four times" since leaving office.

On September 12, 2018, Trump tweeted: "John Kerry had illegal meetings with the very hostile Iranian Regime, which can only serve to undercut our great work to the detriment of the American people. He told them to wait out the Trump Administration! Was he registered under the Foreign Agents Registration Act? BAD!"

Kerry, not being a lobbyist for Iran, was not required to register under FARA. The Logan Act has never been successfully used to prosecute any American since its enactment in 1799.

Kerry responded to Trump's tweet on September 14, 2018, plugging his new book at the same time: "Mr. President, you should be more worried about Paul Manafort meeting with Robert Mueller than me meeting with Iran's FM. But if you want to learn something about the nuclear agreement that made the world safer, buy my new book,

---

[36] Sam Jones, "Ex-NATO chief refused visa waiver to US because of Iran trips," *The Guardian*, June 25, 2018.

Every Day Is Extra." Kerry's tweet came the same day that Manafort agreed to plead guilty to all charges leveled against him by Mueller and promising full cooperation with the office of the special prosecutor.

The nations sanctioned by Trump all fell within his category for such abuse: Trump believed they were all shitholes. If only more Norwegians would move to the United States – something he urged Congress to help facilitate -- would Trump be satisfied about U.S. immigration policy.

Donald "Twitler" and his Restless Twitter Finger

What kind of person, who happens to be in charge of the most destructive nuclear weapons armada in the world, spends the witching hours and mornings tweeting insults and messages more befitting of a petulant juvenile? That person would be the notorious Führer of Twitter, Donald "Twitler" Trump. Journalists, intelligence officers, government officials, and the heads of major multinational corporations were forced to

"follow" Trump on Twitter, just to find out what his daily "warnings and indications" yielded. Even Adolf Hitler, at the height of his and Nazi Propaganda Minister Joseph Goebbel's unrelenting indoctrination campaign carried over cheap radio sets, called *Volksempfängers*, occasionally took a rest from their bombastic tirades.

Like a broken record, Trump's tweets carried the same refrain, over and over, again, *ad nauseum*. Like some of his loyal zombies, Trump often used ALL CAPS to drive home his points. It stands to reason that someone who cannot speak without shouting would use the digital form of shouting in his tweets. For a president of the United States, Trump's repeated poor spelling and capitalizing wrong words would have earned him a flunking grade in elementary school.

Most of Trump's tweets provided an insight into the mind of a completely paranoid criminal. Special prosecutor Mueller and his team of investigators became known as "Mueller and his 17 Angry Democrats" carrying out a "Rigged Witch Hunt." Trump became a virtual cyber-version of the insulting sock puppet, "Triumph the Insult Comic Dog."

On January 6, 2018, after the publication of Michael Wolff's book, *Fire and Fury*, which provided insights into Trump's mental instability, Trump responded in one of his usual Twitter storms: "Actually, throughout my life, my two greatest assets have been mental stability and being, like, really smart. Crooked Hillary Clinton also played these cards very hard and, as everyone knows, went down in flames. I went from VERY successful businessman, to top T.V. Star ..... to President of the United States (on my first try). I think that would qualify as not smart, but genius....and a very stable genius at that!"

"Hey Trump! I'm the only stable genius in history! So, shut up!"

Stable genius? The only "T.V. Star" who could claim that titled was "Mr. Ed," the talking horse of the 1960s sitcom with the same name. Mr. Ed would have told Trump, the bloviating gas bag, "Stop gabbin' and get me some oats!"

What concerned many Americans was the September 2018 announcement by the Federal Emergency Management Agency (FEMA) that it was going to test the "Presidential Alert" system, one of three systems used to notify the public via their cellphones about an emergency situation. The other two types of messages are extreme weather notifications and AMBER Alerts on missing children.

The system was originally scheduled for a test on September 20, 2019, but the date was moved to October 3. The message: "THIS IS A TEST of the National Wireless Emergency Alert System. No action is needed," had no opt-out functionality and was designed to be transmitted over 100 wireless carriers, including Verizon, AT&T, Sprint, and T-Mobile.

Customers immediately voiced their concern that Trump would abuse the system for his own political purposes. The alert messages interrupt any other communications upon transmittal. No one wanted to be alerted with the same type of digital gibberish often sent by Trump in his tweets, for example, "NO COLLUSION! And "WITCH HUNT!" With the emergency alert system, Trump had a powerful *Volksempfänger* at his disposal.

On September 19, 2018, Trump insulted every American with the following mangled tweet: "Our great country has been divided for decades. Sometimes you need protest in order to heel, & we will heel, & be stronger than ever before!"

Trump, who insults people by likening them to "dogs," decided that Americans should "heel." Follow closely the dear leader America! Not a day went by when Trump did not show that he had the intellect of an invertebrate slug.

Although Melania Trump's major policy goal as First Lady was to stop cyber-bullying, her husband was not only one of the chief bullies from his "bully pulpit" at the White House, but he set a bad example for Trumpers and their children. Many were encouraged by their leader to send their own hateful tweets.

On March 2, 2018, Trump, having to deal with issues of war and peace, found time to send a tweet slamming the actor who portrayed him on *Saturday Night Live*, Alec Baldwin (and, he also managed to misspell his name):

"Alex [sic] Baldwin, whose dieing [sic] mediocre career was saved by his impersonation of me on SNL, now says playing DJT was agony for him. Alex, it was also agony for those who were forced to watch. You were terrible. Bring back Darrell Hammond, much funnier and far greater talent!"

It was too bad that Jack Nicholson was not standing next to Trump when he was complaining about Alec Baldwin. Only Nicholson, playing novelist Melvin Udall in *As Good as It Gets*, could have told Trump what many Americans were thinking, especially after being subjected to Trump's inane rants before and during his presidency: "Sell crazy someplace else, we're all stocked up here."

If Trump had been standing in New York's Central Park and yelled out to passers-by what he tweeted on a daily basis, he would have been hauled off in a straight-jacket to the mental health ward at Bellevue Hospital in Manhattan.

Trump's May 29, 2018 tweet resembled that of a paranoid lunatic: "Why aren't the 13 Angry and heavily conflicted Democrats investigating the totally Crooked Campaign of totally Crooked Hillary Clinton. It's a Rigged Witch Hunt, that's why! Ask them if they enjoyed her after election celebration!"

On July 29, 2018, Trump boasted in a tweet that his poll numbers were higher than Abraham Lincoln's. Trump wrote, "Wow, highest Poll Numbers in the history of the Republican Party. That includes Honest Abe Lincoln and

Ronald Reagan." Presidential polling did not begin until 1936, when Gallup first began polling in the election between Franklin D. Roosevelt and his Republican opponent, Alf Landon. In pursuit of transforming the Republican Party into a Trump personality cult vassal organization, Trump had to disparage leading Republican figures of the past, Lincoln and Reagan included.

Before Trump's man-crush on Chairman Kim of the DPRK, he tweeted out the following on November 11, 2017: "Why would Kim Jong-un insult me by calling me "old," when I would NEVER call him "short and fat?" Oh well, I try so hard to be his friend - and maybe someday that will happen!" Well, for Trump his friendship did blossom later blossomed with Kim, however, Trump was still old.

And it was likely Trump's old age and his flagging manhood that resulted in the following tweet-burst on January 2, 2018: "North Korean Leader Kim Jong Un just stated that the 'Nuclear Button is on his desk at all times.' Will someone from his depleted and food starved regime please inform him that I too have a Nuclear Button, but it is a much bigger & more powerful one than his, and my Button works!"

According to Stephanie Clifford, also known as "Stormy Daniels," Trump's porn star hush-money recipient and subsequent accuser, Trump's "button" resembles "Toad the mushroom character in Mario Kart." For the oldsters, Mario Kart is a Nintendo video game. The description of Trump's bizarre "First Member" was revealed in her tell-all book, *Full Disclosure*.

On May 31, 2017, Trump tweeted out one of the more bizarre of his inane tweets: "Despite the constant press covfefe." Intelligence agents around the world scrambled to find out whether "covfefe" was some secret code word for the United States to take some sort of surprise action. Alas, it was merely Trump being his usual dumbshit self. The world rested easy. For only a sort while, however. At 6:09 am on May 31, 2018, Trump sent code breakers around the world back to work, when he tweeted: "Who can figure out the true meaning of "covfefe" ??? Enjoy!

"It Can't Happen Here?" It damned well did happen here!

In the 1935 novel by Sinclair Lewis, *It Can't Happen Here*, a fascist tyrant named Berzelius "Buzz" Windrip is elected president in 1936. Windrip's supporters are sycophantic followers of the man they simply call "Buzz." Buzz supporters are enraptured by his false promises and his constant fusillade of bald-faced lies. Buzz promises his supporters he will crack down on Mexico – he ends up launching an invasion of Mexico -- and deal harshly with the bankers. Buzz's rhetoric about Mexico and Trump's promise to build a wall on the U.S.-Mexican border were eerily similar. The "wall" became a constant subject of Trump's spastic-like tweets, including, "Our Southern Border is under siege. Congress must act now to change our weak and ineffective immigration laws. Must build a Wall."

Building a wall on the U.S.-Mexican border was a hallmark of Trump's campaign and his presidency. He constantly railed against Mexicans as gang members, rapists, and drug dealers. Vicente Fox, who served as Mexico's president from 2000 to 2006 had the following to say about the wall on CNBC: "The building of a wall is the stupidity out of the mind of Trump," adding, "It's just isolating the United States from the rest of the world."[37] However, Trump wanted to isolate the U.S. from the rest of the world. It was a re-play of the pro-Nazi "America First" movement from the 1930s.

In January 2017, Fox laid down a gauntlet to Trump, who had campaigned on the theme of making Mexico pay for his wall. Fox tweeted: "I am not paying for that fucking wall." Fox became an instant hero on both sides of the U.S.-Mexican border.

It Can't Happen Here had other eerie predictions of life in a fascist America. "Communists" in Windrip's America are imprisoned in concentration camps or executed as traitors. Jews only become certified as "fully Americanized," so long as they pledge allegiance to Windrip's policies.

An underground movement forms in the United States and one of its chief leaders is a journalist named Doremus Jessup. As Donald Trump declared members of the press to be "enemies of the people," many Doremus Jessups arose, willing to confront Trump on his lies and blatant propaganda. Some paid with their lives.

Trump, like other autocrats, clearly rejected the trappings of a democracy. Trump demanded total loyalty from the Department of Justice and security apparatuses like the

---

[37] Matthew Belvedere, "Ex-Mexican President Vicente Fox: The idea of a border wall is 'stupidity out of the mind of Trump,'" CNBC, April 23, 2018.

FBI and he set about on a course to purge them of anyone who failed to toe his political line. Trump also rejected the independence of the federal courts and sought to pack federal benches with unqualified sycophants, the worst being U.S. Court of Appeals Judge for the District of Columbia, the beer-loving Brett Kavanaugh.

An incident in June 2018 demonstrated what sort of tight ship Trump ran. While flying aboard Air Force One, Trump took a call from someone he believed was Senator Robert Menendez (D-NJ). In fact, the caller was John Melendez, who was a former regular on the Howard Stern radio show, which had also featured Trump as a guest. Melendez spoofed White House staff and convinced them he was Menendez.

The call revealed that Trump was sympathetic to the federal corruption charges against Menendez, which were dropped after a hung jury failed to reach a consensus on a guilty determination. Trump, who is a walking and talking corruption magnet, told Menendez, "You went through a tough, tough situation - and I don't think a very fair situation - but congratulations."[38] One could be forgiven if they thought they were listening to dialogue from *The Sopranos*.

An independent and co-equal legislative branch, crafted by

---

[38] Adam S. Levy and Chris Spargo, "Trump is prank called by comedian 'Stuttering John' Melendez pretending to be a US Democratic senator and discusses his zero-tolerance policy and Supreme Court pick," *Daily Mail*, June 29, 2018.

the founders of the United States as a check on the powers of the presidency, was something that got under Trump's skin. Republican senators and representatives who so wildly cheered Trump's nationalistic and jingoistic 2018 State of the Union address reminded one of the statement of the character, Senator Padme Amidala (Natalie Portman), in the *Star Wars* episode, *Revenge of the Sith*. Padme, witnessing the reception of her fellow senators to Chancellor Palpatine's plan to seize power and change the Galactic Republic into an imperial dictatorship, declared, "So this is how liberty dies . . . with thunderous applause." Those Republicans and even a few Democratic quislings who applauded and cheered the autocrat Trump during the State of the Union address became witting participants in Trump's desire to create a rump parliament in the place of the U.S. Congress.

The term "rump parliament" comes from the latter days of the Second English Civil War. In December 1648, Colonel Thomas Pride blocked entry to the English Parliament of 231 supporters of the Treaty of Newport, which was designed to restore King Charles I to the throne. Only those members of parliament who opposed the treaty were permitted to sit in parliament as virtual rubber stamps for the tyrannical Commonwealth of England, a dictatorship that would soon fall under the total control of the theocratic despot Oliver Cromwell. In 1653, even the rump parliamentarians became a hindrance to Cromwell, so he had the rump parliament completely dissolved.

The English rump parliament was copied by dictatorships

around the world. These "remnant" legislatures, which were kept in place following a seizure of power by a tyrant, were all designed to give the appearance of democratic rule when, in fact, they were nothing more than window-dressing contrivances and applause machines for dictators and autocrats.

Rump parliaments, or undemocratic legislatures, have existed in several Communist countries and fascist dictatorships. Perhaps the most undemocratic of these has been the Supreme People's Assembly of the Democratic People's Republic of Korea. Whenever this North Korean rump parliament met, it was to wildly cheer and applaud speeches by the three generations of Kim family leaders: Kim Il Sung, Kim Jong Il, and Kim Jong Un. Donald Trump can only be envious of the Kims for having such a compliant legislature.

After the 1973 Chilean coup by General Augusto Pinochet the military junta disposed of the bicameral Chilean Senate and Chamber of Deputies altogether. The junta served as the executive and legislature until 1990. The pre-1997 Mexican presidents, all members of the dominant Institutional Revolutionary Party (PRI), relied on a subservient legislature to carry out their policies.

On June 28, 2018, one of Trump's "bananas" supporters, Jarrod W. Ramos, a Laurel, Maryland resident who had an eight year-long crazy feud with a local newspaper, *The Annapolis Capital-Gazette*, felt emboldened by Trump's anti-press attacks to commit a horrible act of violence in the newsroom of the paper. Five members of the newspaper staff were killed. They were columnist and assistant editor Rob Hiaasen, the brother of famed Florida-based author and journalist Carl Hiaasen; special publications editor Wendi Winters; editorial page editor Gerald Fischman; sports reporter John McNamara; and assistant Rebecca Smith.

Ramos was a constant Twitterer and he used the social media platform to defend Trump and a local former Anne Arundel County supervisor and Southern secessionist named Michael Peroutka. In a tweet sent on September 16, 2015, during Trump's initial campaign for the presidency, Ramos warned the *Capital-Gazette* that their reference to Trump being "unqualified could *end badly* (again)." [emphasis added]

Earlier, Ramos appeared to praise the January 7, 2015 terrorist attack on the French satirical magazine *Charlie Hebdo*. Twelve members of the Paris-based magazine's staff were killed in the shooting spree attributed to Islamic State. In another tweet, Ramos warned that he was "suing the shit out of half of AA [Anne Arundel] County and making *corpses* [emphasis added] of current careers and corporate entities."

Ramos tweeted on March 11, 2015, about Shaun Adamec, the press secretary for former Maryland Democratic Governor Martin O'Malley, stating that, "dying is a touchy subject for him." Referring to Adamec as a "bad journalist," Ramos told him, "just go about your business as Clinton's press secretary." There is no record of Adamec ever having worked as a press secretary for either Bill or Hillary Clinton. After Ramos's attack on the Annapolis newspaper, his past Twitter threats against the *Baltimore Sun* resulted in police conducting a search of the paper's offices in downtown Baltimore. The New York Police Department, fearing copy-cat attacks, provided security to at least a dozen media offices in the city, including the offices of *The New York Times,* a frequent recipient of Trump's attacks.

Nashville police provided added security for the *Tennessean*. The Chicago police monitored security at the *Chicago Tribune* and *Chicago Sun-Times*. Los Angeles police beefed up security at the *Los Angeles Times*. A Trump supporter called in a veiled threat to the *Standard-Examiner* in Ogden, Utah. The typical "Bananas Republicans" tried to push back against clear evidence that Ramos was spurred into action by Trump's rhetoric, but their defense was pathetic.

Ramos was of the same ilk as California resident Robert D. Chain, who, on September 30, 2018, the same day the National Press Club in Washington honored the staff of the *Capital-Gazette*, was arrested by federal agents in Encino, California and charged with threatening to kill the employees of *The Boston Globe* in a mass shooting at their headquarters at 1 Exchange Place in downtown Boston. Like Ramos, Chain believed that he was carrying out Trump's wishes by attacking the press, what Trump repeatedly called the "enemy of the people." Trump's perverse use of the presidential "bully pulpit: to encourage actual and would-be murderers of journalists represented the lowest of the low in American politics.

In January 2018, Taylor Wilson, a neo-Nazi from Missouri, who attended the "United the Right" rally in Charlottesville, was arrested for threatening an attack on CNN's headquarters in Atlanta. In October 2017, Taylor Wilson hit the emergency brake on an Amtrak train in the middle of Nebraska. Wilson told police, "I stopped the fucking train . . . I was going to save the train from the black people."[39] Wilson was an adherent of the Covenant Nation Church of Oneonta, Alabama. The church's pastor, William Davidson, believes that white people are among the Lost Ten Tribes of Israel. The church should have checked to see who was spiking the watermelons with booze at the church's picnics.

In July 2018, a man named Andrew Angel, attacked a Hispanic man who was sitting in his car, which was parked outside of a Starbuck's in the town of Countryside, Illinois southwest of Chicago. Angel had tried to put a flier bearing a Nazi swastika on the man's car. After the Hispanic man declined the Nazi flier, Angel launched into a racial tirade, calling the man a "spic motherfucker." When police searched Angel's car, they found Nazi and Confederate flags, a Ku Klux Klan hood, white nationalist literature, and

---

[39] Chris Riotta, "Neo-Nazi pleads guilty to terrorism charge after 'trying to save train from black people,'" *The Independent*, July 13, 2018.

a ventriloquist dummy.[40] Imagine, a Nazi version of Edgar Bergen and Charlie McCarthy! Had it been Trump, instead of Angel, arrested, Donald would have undoubtedly tried to blame the verbal assault on the dummy.

It was painfully obvious from whom such right-wing loons and terrorists got their crackpot ideas: the bellicose petit-tyrant in the White House.

There was no telling where Trump's anti-press rhetoric would end. In 2017, Omar Perez, a clearly delusional individual, who claimed assailants were invading his "private life by tapping into the electronic devices and feeding off attachments such as audio speakers and digital cameras," filed suit in U.S. Court in Cincinnati. Judge Karen Litkovitz called Perez's suit "rambling, difficult to decipher [which] borders on delusional."

On September 6, 2018, Perez walked into the lobby of Fifth Third Center in downtown Cincinnati and opened fire. Three people were killed and two were wounded. Perez's paranoid beef was with the CNBC business news network and TD Ameritrade. The question had to be asked: Was Trump setting off people with severe psychological conditions to attack the press? Did Trump make any effort to tamp down his demagogic characterization of the press? Not one damned bit. And by the end of September 2018, it was a damned sure thing that others, as crazed as

---

[40] Lorraine Swanson, "Alleged Neo-Nazi Ventriloquist Charged With Starbucks Hate Crime, Patch.com, July 24, 2018.

Ramos, Chain, and Perez, were lying in wait for unsuspecting journalists.

Trump had previously put a target on several newspapers and periodicals he tweeted were "dying," "failing," "pure scum," "clowns," or "stupid." These included *The New Hampshire Union Leader*, *The New York Daily News*, *The New York Times*, *The Washington Post*, *The Wall Street Journal*, *Vanity Fair*, and *Politico*.

During a September 2018 rally in Billings, Montana, Trump cheered on the incumbent GOP congressman's assault of Ben Jacobs, a reporter for *The Guardian* of the UK, during the 2016 campaign. Representative Greg Gianforte pleaded guilty to criminal charge of assault. Nevertheless, Trump said, referring to Gianforte's body slamming the reporter and then lying about it to police, said, "This man has fought—in more ways than one—for your state. He is a fighter and a winner."[41]

There was little wonder why newsrooms and broadcast centers across the country had been forced to higher extra security. *The New York Times's* publisher, A. G. Sulzberger, told Trump at a July20, 2018 meeting at the White House that more than the president's use of the pejorative term "fake news," his labeling of the press as "the enemy of the people" was far more worrying. Sulzberger said, "I warned that this inflammatory language is contributing to a rise in

---

[41] Matthew Zeitlin, "At Rally, Trump Praises Physical Violence, Warns Impeachment Could Turn U.S. Into "Third World Country," Slate, September 7, 2018.

threats against journalists and will lead to violence." Later, Trump, in a tweet, lied about the subject of his meeting with Sulzberger, stating the meeting was about "the vast amounts of Fake News being put out by the media & how that Fake News has morphed into phrase, 'Enemy of the People.' Sad!"[42]

What was sad was an ignorant asshole like Trump being ignorant of the fact that American journalists had died trying to bring news reports about issues of war and peace to the American people. One of the first recorded incidents of a journalist being killed in the line of duty was Elijah Paris Lovejoy, the abolitionist editor of the *Alton Observer* in Alton, Illinois. Lovejoy was killed in 1827 by a pro-slavery mob. Remember, Trump said there were "fine people" on both sides of the neo-Confederate and white supremacy mob scene in Charlottesville, Virginia.

Don Mellett of the *Canton Daily News* in Ohio was shot to death in 1927 at his home for covering a story involving corruption between a mob chief and the police chief. If he was president in 1927, Trump would call such an exposé of high-level corruption involving government officials and criminals, "fake news."

On June 2, 1976, Don Bolles of the *Arizona Republic*, was assassinated in a car bomb explosion. Bolles was killed for exposing high-level mafia connections to Arizona race

---

[42] Mark Landler, "New York Times Publisher and Trump Clash Over President's Threats Against Journalism," *The New York Times*, July 29, 2018.

tracks and the Frontier Hotel and Casino in Las Vegas. An irony or all ironies is that Trump built his Trump Hotel Las Vegas on part of the property occupied by the mobbed-up Frontier casino. The Frontier was razed in 2007 to make way for the Trump building.

Thomas Pecorelli, a freelance photojournalist, was killed on September 11, 2001. He was a passenger on board American Airlines flight 11 that was crashed into the North Tower of the World Trade Center in Manhattan.

The sacrifices of these and other journalists killed while covering wars, including reporters like Ernie Pyle of Scripps-Howard (World War II), George Polk of CBS (Greek Civil War), Sam Castan of *Look* magazine, Charles Eggleston of UPI, Paul Savanuck of *Stars and Stripes*, Kent Potter of UPI, Alexander Shimkin of *Newsweek* (Vietnam), Welles Hangen of NBC and George Syvertsen of CBS (Cambodian war), Daniel Pearl of *The Wall Street Journal* (South Asian war against Al Qaeda), and David Bloom of NBC (Iraq war), are not appreciated by a vapid pant load like Trump.

Trump has the nerve to call journalists the "enemy of the people" and their reports "fake news" in the shadow of the ultimate sacrifices made by American and journalists around the world. There are insufficient epithets in the English language to describe a thoroughly despicable scoundrel like Trump. It was bad enough that the alt-right of white supremacists and neo-Nazis targeted journalists for violent acts, including murder. What was as astounding was the fact that some within this ilk wanted to be members of the U.S. House, Senate, and other high elective office.

The following were just a few of these racist Republican knuckleheads:

- Patrick Little, candidate for U.S. Senate from California. Advocated a ban on immigration into U.S., except for "biological kin." Also declared that no person of Jewish origin should "live, vacation, or traverse in the U.S."

- Arthur Jones, U.S. House candidate, 3rd congressional district, Illinois. Attended rallies commemorating Adolf Hitler's birth. Worked closely with the Ku Klux Klan and Aryan Nations.

- Paul Nehlen, U.S. House candidate, 1st congressional district, Wisconsin). Advocated killing immigrants at the U.S. southern border. Also favored assassination of his political opponents.

- Corey Stewart, U.S. Senate candidate, Virginia. Supported neo-Confederate movement, white supremacists, and neo-Nazis.

- Sean Donohue U.S. House candidate, 11th congressional district, Pennsylvania). Associated with former Ku Klux Klan leader David Duke.

- Seth Grossman, U.S. House candidate, 2nd congressional district, New Jersey. Endorsed white nationalist websites and called Islam a "cancer."

- John Fitzgerald, U.S. House candidate, 11th congressional district, California. Appeared on neo-Nazi podcasts and claimed the Holocaust was a "lie."

- Steve West, candidate, Missouri House District 15, said "Hitler was right about what was taking place in Germany."

Granted, none of these candidates was given a chance to win their primary or general election races. Others, also on the alt-right fringe, were running for major office.

Included in this lot was Representative Ron DeSantis of Florida, who was running for governor, an election that -- to Florida's everlasting shame -- was successful for DeSantis. The day after winning the GOP nomination, DeSantis told Fox News that his Democratic opponent, Andrew Gillum, the African-American mayor of Tallahassee, would, if elected "monkey this up," meaning the state of Florida. DeSantis's supporters denied he was using a familiar racist dog whistle. However, DeSantis's record as a congressman was not all that different from that of Steve King, the Iowa congressman, who also enjoyed the company of the ghouls of the alt-right.

Earlier, DeSantis referred to Democratic U.S. House candidate from New York, Alexandria Ocasio-Cortez, who is of Puerto Rican descent, as a "whatever she is." From November 16 to 19, 2017, DeSantis attended the "Restoration Weekend" conference at the Breakers Resort in Palm Beach, Florida, just over the intercoastal waterway from Trump's Mar-A-Lago parasite- and mold-infested exclusive "resort."[43]

The weekend retreat, an annual gathering of Islamophobes sponsored by hate monger David Horowitz, featured as speakers, in addition to DeSantis, Steve Bannon, Sebastian Gorka, whacko cable news pundit Ann Coulter, and alt-right idol Milo Yiannopoulos. It was not DeSantis's first time appearing at a dais with Gorka. In February 2018, DeSantis appeared with the Hungarian version of Dr. Strangelove at a St. Lucie County, Florida Lincoln Day Dinner.

Two of DeSantis's House GOP colleagues joined him at the hate fest. They were Brian Mast of Florida and Devin Nunes, the chairman of the House Intelligence Committee. Nothing said "major U.S. intelligence security breach" more than Devin Nunes, a participant in a conference that was packed with neo-Nazis and white supremacists. If Nunes were a member of the military or any of America's intelligence services, such attendance would have earned him a quick revocation of his access to classified material.

---

[43] Mar-A-Lago was cited 78 times by Florida health inspectors. Violations included "smoked salmon being served without undergoing proper parasite destruction," a meat slicer "soiled with old food debris," an ice machine with an "accumulation of a black/green mold-like substance." Trump hosted for meals at his gold-plated dump Japanese Prime Minister Shinzo Abe and Chinese President Xi Jinping. Trump boasted that he and Xi shared a "beautiful" chocolate cake while the two dined at Mar-A-Lago in April 2017. Perhaps, Trump should have been informed that the 1972 U.S. signing of the Biological Weapons Convention prohibited him from serving toxic food to the leaders of China and Japan, both signatories of the convention.

Also present at Restoration Weekend was British anti-Muslim blogger Katie Hopkins, who advocated putting Muslims into internment camps. As seen with the detention in "tender care centers" of young children, torn from their asylum-seeking parents at the U.S. southern border, the alt-right, whether in the United States or Europe, has an affectation for concentration camps.

Not even Nazi Germany forced toddlers, some as young as three-years old, to appear in court -- representing themselves after being separated from their parents -- at immigration deportation hearings. But, thanks to the wanna-be Nazi, Stephen Miller, this travesty actually occurred at immigration courts in Texas and California. Miller's desire to emulate Nazi commander Adolf Eichmann may have been due to what his third-grade school teacher in Los Angeles revealed was his problem. Nikki Fiske, Miller's teacher, said Miller would pour glue on to his arm, wait for it to dry, peel it off, and then eat it.[44] It was too bad that Miller put the glue on his arm. His lips would have been a better option, but only had he used permanent super glue.

The theme of this book is to poke fun at the comedic antics of the buffoon Trump. One thing that definitely was

---

[44] Benjamin Svetkey, "Stephen Miller's Third-Grade Teacher: He Was a 'Loner' and Ate Glue," *The Hollywood Reporter*, October 10, 2018.

not humorous about Trump was what befell young children and their parents on the U.S. southern border.

The locations of young girls and toddlers ripped apart from their parents and detained in separate facilities across the United States, were not initially disclosed by either U.S. Immigration and Customs Enforcement (ICE) or the Department of Health and Human Services (DHHS). The latter had been tasked with running several detention centers around the country, however, many of the detention facilities were operated by private prison contractors known for providing sub-standard services to inmates.

Several media operations reported that while they were given closely-supervised tours of detention centers housing boys, they were not allowed to tour any facilities where girls and toddlers were sent. This gave rise to a question throughout the country -- "where are the girls and babies?"

The question took on added meaning in a country whose president had a rap sheet that strongly suggested he and his peers had, in the past, sexually abused children. The incidents involving Trump included the alleged rapes of 12- and 13-year old girls at convicted child sex abuser Jeffrey Epstein's Manhattan townhouse in 1994 and other children at Trump's Mar-a-Lago estate in Palm Beach, Florida, Trump Tower in New York, and a Trump vineyard estate in Charlottesville, Virginia.

On August 1, 2018, Trump's sordid history around young girls elicited the following limerick from yours truly:

*"There once was a pervert from Queens
Who liked raping very young teens
Unable for an erection
He sought the election
As president through unlawful means."*

Trump endorsed GOP Senate candidate Roy Moore of Alabama in a December 2017 special election to fill Jeff Sessions's seat. Moore had been accused of sexually accosting underage girls when he was an Alabama county prosecutor in his early 30s. Trump publicly accused Moore's accusers, some who were younger than 15 years old at the time of Moore's alleged sexual advances, of lying. Trump would repeat the charge that other women, those who accused Trump's Supreme Court nominee Brett Kavanaugh of sexual assault when they were in high school, were lying.

Trump could always be found on the wrong side of the law: whether the crime was sexual assault of minors, tax evasion, criminal conspiracy, and racketeering. There was a reason why Trump took up for criminals, including the infamous gangster Al Capone. Trump knew he had engaged in the same sort of criminal activity as those he consistently defended.

In the 1930s, America saw large meetings of far-rightists. These were sponsored by the German-American Bund, a more genteel name for what was, in reality, the American Nazi Party. One can strongly believe that someone like Trump's dad, Fred Trump, Sr., just may have been one of the 20,000 Nazi-saluting Bund members at a massive Nazi rally at Madison Square Garden in Manhattan in 1939.

Most of what the world knows about Fred Trump, the

ethnic German father of President Donald Trump, falls between 1927, when he was arrested at a Ku Klux Klan riot in Queens, in the pre-war 1930s when he built and managed several rental homes around Queens on behalf of his E. Trump & Son real estate development company, and the post-war years, when his Trump Management Company operated several apartment buildings and housing developments. Around New York City, Fred Trump's real estate mini-empire benefited from generous financing from the Federal Housing Administration. However, the years during World War II remain as a sketchy, suspicious, and nebulous gap in Fred Trump's "official" biography.

Fred, who misrepresented himself and his family as being of Swedish and not German descent, fit the profile of a Nazi "sleeper agent." Fred was more than happy to bid on U.S. Navy contracts to build barracks and cottage homes at naval yards in Chester, Pennsylvania and Newport News and Norfolk, Virginia. The ports also happened to be the disembarkation points for thousands of newly-trained U.S.

and Canadian troops shipping off the Europe to fight the Axis. Troop ship convoy schedules constituted highly-prized intelligence for German U-Boats lurking off the U.S. east coast.

On its fateful last voyage in 1936, the German airship *Hindenburg* made it a point to fly over numerous cities and towns in the New York-New Jersey-Philadelphia corridor that had high German-American concentrations as a propaganda display.

Fred Trump's FHA-funded apartment complex in Coney Island was so infamous for its policy of refusing to rent to blacks, even black veterans of the war, that Woody Guthrie, who lived in the tenement from 1950 to 1952, wrote a song titled "Old Man Trump." Little did Woody, the father of Arlo Guthrie, know, that the son of "Old Man Trump" would not only become president of the United States, but its first openly pro-Nazi president.

Guthrie's song goes as follows:

"I suppose that Old Man Trump knows just how much racial hate
He stirred up in that bloodpot of human hearts
When he drawed that color line
Here at his Beach Haven family project

Beach Haven ain't my home!
No, I just can't pay this rent!
My money's down the drain,
And my soul is badly bent!
Beach Haven is Trump's Tower
Where no black folks come to roam,

No, no, Old Man Trump!
Old Beach Haven ain't my home!"

In 1973, the federal government took Fred and his apprenticeship son Donald to court over their violation of the Fair Housing Act of 1968.

Trump's father funneled to Donald some $413 million in today's money, nowhere near the $1 million loan Donald Trump claimed his father loaned him and which, he paid back with interest. It turned out that old man Trump gamed the tax code to steer millions of dollars to sonny boy through a network of limited liability corporations, partnerships, and trusts. Fred Trump also provided laundry money from his residential apartment buildings to Donald.[45] It was an actual case of laundering laundry money!

This same sort of interconnected business network, involving domestic and foreign limited liability corporations, trusts, shell corporations, and partnerships, would serve as a contrivance for Donald Trump, Sr.; his sons Donald Trump, Jr. and Eric Trump (better known as "Uday and Qusay" or "Beavis and Butthead"); his daughter Ivanka Trump and her husband, Jared Kushner; and associates like lawyer Michael Cohen, Trump propagandist

---

[45] David Barstow, Susanne Craig, and Russ Buettner, "Trump Engaged in Suspect Tax Schemes as He Reaped Riches from His Father," *The New York Times*, October 2, 2018.

Sean Hannity of Fox News; Commerce Secretary Wilbur Ross; and several other Trump cronies.

On November 11, 2018, Trump failed to show up at a ceremony at the Aisne-Marne American Cemetery and Memorial, adjacent to the Belleau Wood battlefield, some 60 miles outside of Paris. Over 2000 American doughboys and Marines lost their lives in the battle. The ceremony, skipped by Trump due to what he erroneously called "bad weather," marked the 100th anniversary of the World War I armistice.

Ivanka Trump showed her disdain for America's war dead on Memorial Day in 2017. She tweeted: "Make champagne popsicles this #MemorialDay." Nothing says honoring those who sacrificed their lives in America's past wars than champagne popsicles. The Trump family record shows that none of the Trump's ever served in the military. Trump's grandfather avoided conscription in his native Germany by fleeing to North America; Trump's father, Fred, avoided the draft in World War II, even though he was of age; and Donald Trump avoided the draft during Vietnam by claiming a medical deferment resulting from "bone spurs." As for Donald Jr. and Eric Trump, their idea of carrying a weapon is to shoot endangered animals in Africa.

It is significant, in view of how far to the right the Republican Party became, that it was the Nixon administration that took the Trumps to court. The suit was settled in 1975 with no admission of guilt by the Trumps. That stance was courtesy of Donald's then-mentor, the Joe McCarthy Red-baiting counsel Roy Cohn, a vicious anti-Semitic Jew and self-hating homosexual. Cohn convinced Donald Trump to counter-sue the Nixon administration.

The attempt failed but Trump learned that Cohn's advice to sue anyone at the drop of a hat would serve him well in the future.

Trump, in bouts of despair over his legal problems, often bemoaned the fact that he had no "Roy Cohn" to attack his enemies. Trump wrongly believed that his Attorney General, Jeff Sessions, would be his "Roy Cohn." When that was not in the cards, Trump fired Sessions, replacing him as acting Attorney General, quite outside the normal line of succession, with Sessions's chief of staff, Matthew Whitaker.

Whitaker, a former U.S. Attorney in Iowa during the Bush 43 administration, was also a scam artist for dubious companies, including World Patent Marketing of Miami Beach. Whitaker, who served on the firm's board, helped market a deep toilet designed so that "well-endowed" men did not have to worry about their genitals from making contact with the water. Whitaker also claimed that DNA evidence proved the existence of Big Foot. It was part of a pitch to market Sasquatch dolls. Whitaker also helped pitch the firm's Time Travel X project, a scam involving theoretical time travel and investments in Bitcoin.[46]

Who wouldn't want a time machine? Just think. If one could travel back to the early 1930s and prevent Fred

---

[46] Geoff Herbert, "Acting AG Matt Whitaker under fire for alleged Bigfoot, toilet, time travel scams," Syracuse.com, November 15, 2018.

Trump from meeting Scottish housemaid, Mary MacLeod, at a dance in New York, a certain bloviating orange menace would have never been born. But more on Donald Trump, Biff Tannen and *Back to the Future* a little later.

Based on Donald Trump's fascination with a book of Adolf Hitler's collected speeches, *My New Order*, which Trump's first wife Ivana claimed he kept on the nightstand, next to his bed, questions certainly arose about Fred's actual loyalties during the war against Nazi Germany. Although Fred's parents were German immigrants and Fred was conceived in the "Fatherland," Fred lied about his German roots during and after World War II. Why? Was he covering up a deep secret from the FBI, which was always on the lookout for German sleeper agents during the war? Fred Trump's KKK activities in Queens, during the late 1920s, while Hitler's nascent Nazi Party was becoming a political force to be reckoned with in Germany, were also very suspicious.

Old man Trump probably had no idea that on May 6, 1937, as the German airship *Hindenburg* -- adorned with its Nazi swastikas for all to see -- flew over Manhattan on its last voyage before exploding in New Jersey, that another flaming Nazi gas bag, his son, would one day be sworn in as president of the United States.

Ironically, old man Trump, the 1927 KKK rally participant and the man with the unusually blank dossier from the 1930s and 40s, died in 1999 at the Long Island Jewish Medical Center in New Hyde Park, Queens.

In an interview with *Vanity Fair*, Trump's first wife, Ivana Trump, was once asked by Trump's mother, Mary Trump, (an immigrant to the United States from Scotland), "What kind of son have I created?"[47] Considering the apple did not fall far from the tree, the answer to that question was more in the purview of Fred Trump, Sr., a 1930s and 40s "man of mystery."

---

[47] Marie Brenner, "After the Gold Rush," *Vanity Fair*, September 1, 1990.

GOP: From the Party of Lincoln to the Party of Grifters, Flat Earthers, Flim-Flam Artists, and Shysters

Donald Trump's current and past business dealings revealed that the real estate tycoon effectively served as a syndicate "Godfather" for some three decades. In 2009, when Ivanka Trump married Jared Kushner, the scion of the Kushner real estate family, the marriage was more of a business merger between the Trump and Kushner business empires. The title of "Godfather" of the sprawling Trump-Kushner real estate empire fell to Donald Trump, particularly after Kushner Companies founder Charles Kushner, the father of Jared, racked up a sizable federal criminal record for illegal campaign contributions, tax evasion, and witness tampering. After Charles Kushner "went away" for "three hots-and-a-cot" with the U.S. Bureau of Prisons, Jared took over the reins of the firm.

A detailed investigation of Trump-Kushner business connections reveals a global web, rife with convicted criminals, money launderers, international smugglers, felons operating under aliases, stock manipulators, bank embezzlers, and blood diamond merchants. Most of these grifters and gangsters were Eurasian Jews, many of whom emigrated to the United States, Britain, and Israel before and after the collapse of the Soviet Union. Brooklyn became a nexus for what the FBI alternately referred to as "Eurasian Organized Crime Syndicates" or "Russian Organized Crime Syndicates." The first demonstration of Jared Kushner's influence in the Trump administration occurred during the presidential transition. This was evident in the firing from the transition team of its chairman, New Jersey Governor Chris Christie and his loyalists, which included former U.S. Representative Mike Rogers and Matthew Freedman.

For Jared, the firings were a Mafia-like payback. While U.S. Attorney for Northern New Jersey, Christie successfully prosecuted Kushner's father for tax evasion, witness tampering, and illegal campaign contributions. Christie wanted a three-year prison sentence for the elder Kushner, but he ended up serving one year at a federal penitentiary in Alabama.[48] It is for that reason that Jared began pushing for criminal sentencing reform. He hated to travel to Alabama to see daddy in lockup. Of course, Jared couldn't give a shit about all the African-Americans, Hispanics, poor whites, and others run into the U.S. prison-industrial complex for non-violent crimes.

Charles Kushner was not the only criminal in the Kushner family, and, by marriage, the extended Trump family. Jared's uncle, Richard Stadtmauer, the brother of Jared's mother, Seryl Kushner, was convicted in 2009 of federal tax evasion. In 2016, the feds launched an investigation of the defrauding of the New York prison guards' union

---

[48] Wayne Madsen, "Blackmail is specialty of Ivanka Trump's father-in-law," WayneMadsenReport.com, November 17-21, 2016.

through a Stadtmauer/Kushner Companies-financed hedge fund called Platinum Partners. The hedge fund operated in the same manner as Bernard Madoff's company, even using Cayman Islands-based "feeder accounts" -- a fancy name for money laundering operations.

Platinum Partners was investigated by federal prosecutors in Brooklyn, some of whom later joined the staff of Justice Department Special Counsel Robert Mueller. Mueller was reportedly investigating Jared Kushner's role in several questionable financial dealings, including the bilking of investors by Platinum Partners.

In fact, there was a connection between Platinum Partners and Madoff Investment Securities. Both businesses were discovered to be defrauding the Jay Cohen Revocable Trust. Although Jared Kushner and Ivanka Trump claim to be devout Orthodox Jews, Platinum Partners was allegedly defrauding the National Society for Hebrew Day Schools. Charles Kushner, Richard Stadtmauer, and Stadtmauer friend Murray Huberfeld were investors in the Kushner-controlled NorCrown Bank. In 2005, Kushner was ordered to divest himself of all interests in the Livingston, New Jersey-based bank after he was cited for violating federal banking laws. Jared Kushner also maintained a banking role, as witnessed by his sizable interest in another closely-held Kushner-linked bank in Livingston, Regal Bank.

The federal investigation of Kushner Companies and Stadtmauer in 2009 discovered that Kushner officials and Stadtmauer formed several limited partnerships to illegally evade taxes. Court documents showed that several business entities, including those in Jared Kushner's Office of Government Ethics financial disclosure form, were cited for tax evasion, including Westminster Management LLC, Oakwood Garden Associates LLC, and Elmwood Village Associates LP.

Kushner, who filed several versions of his disclosure form because of errors, appeared to still be willfully hiding some assets. According to federal court documents from the 2009 prosecution of Kushner Companies and Stadtmauer, other limited partnerships involved in tax evasion were listed as part of Kushner assets, but were not listed by Jared Kushner in his amended ethics form disclosures. The omitted partnerships were Pheasant Hollow LP, Mt. Arlington LP, QEM LP, and six partnerships with variations of the name Quail Ridge. Purposely failing to include required information on a federal form is a criminal offense and Kushner had at least three opportunities to correct and amend his financial disclosure form.

Donald Trump's international investments were no less troubling. They involved a number of Eurasian oligarchs wanted by Interpol, the FBI, and other law enforcement agencies for everything from bank embezzlement and money laundering to contracted murder and bribery of foreign government officials. Trump's foray into Macau casinos put the president into the murky world of Chinese Triad criminal syndicates.

Trump assuming the presidency is similar to Oswald Cobblepot, also known as The Penguin, being elected mayor of Gotham City. In the television series *Gotham*,

Cobblepot runs on the slogan, "Make Gotham Safe Again." Sort of sounds familiar. Like Trump's "Make America Safe Again." Trump's Cabinet looks like Mayor Cobblepot's administration of Gotham. The Penguin found jobs in the Gotham administration for all of his friends in the Secret Society of Super-Villains: the Joker, the Riddler, Catwoman, and Mr. Freeze. Gotham Police Commissioner James Gordon and Police Chief Clancy O'Hara, like Deputy Attorney General Rod Rosenstein and FBI director James Comey, found their new "bosses" to be their old organized crime enemies. Unlike the fictional Gotham City, there was no Batman to save us from Trump's Society of Super-Villains, although special counsel Robert Mueller came darn close to fitting the bill.

The way Trump fired Comey was the same way the Penguin sacked Chief O'Hara, with malice and total disdain. Comey first learned of his sacking by Trump while attending a minority recruiting conference being held at the Directors Guild of America building in Hollywood, California. Comey actually discovered he had been fired by reading from a crawl that flashed across a television screen. He first believed it was some sort of prank. Comey huddled with FBI officials before darting off to his FBI jet at Los Angeles International Airport and his flight back to DC.

Acting FBI director Andrew McCabe, meanwhile, dispatched FBI agents to seize and seal Comey's office. When Richard Nixon ordered Watergate special prosecutor Archibald Cox fired on October 20, 1973, his Attorney General, Elliot Richardson, and Deputy Attorney General, William Ruckelshaus, refused to carry out the sacking and resigned. Nixon ordered armed federal agents to seize control of the offices of Cox, Richardson, and Ruckelshaus. However, Richardson and Ruckelshaus were smart enough to remove all Watergate-related files from their offices.

It is not known whether Comey removed files related to the investigation of Trump and his campaign but it is clear that Trump took advantage of Comey being on the West Coast to make his move in ousting the FBI director.

In Argentina, President Mauricio Macri, an old business partner of Trump and a billionaire in his own right, became enmeshed in the Odebrecht scandal. That was not good news for Trump. Odebrecht is a Brazilian construction giant, whose foreign bribery operations toppled a president of Brazil, resulted in an indictment of a past Brazilian president of Brazil and an indictment of the incumbent president of the Brazil. The bribery scandal implicated another friend of Trump, former Panamanian president Ricardo Martinelli, who was arrested in Miami pending his ultimate extradition to Panama. Martinelli was a partner in the Ocean Club International Hotel and Tower in Panama City, Panama.

YY Development Group, a firm linked to Macri, was Trump's partner in building a prospective Trump Tower in Buenos Aires, a project that failed to materialize. With Macri imperiled by the Odebrecht bribery scandal and Martinelli imprisoned in Panama, awaiting trial, there was a good reason behind Mueller's hiring of former federal prosecutor Greg Andres as a lawyer on his team.

Andres prosecuted Allen Stanford for running an $8 billion Ponzi scheme centered around Stanford International Bank of Antigua and Barbuda, which also operated in Panama. It emerged that Macri's Argentine construction operations were financed via the Meini Bank, an Austrian bank subsidiary based in Antigua and Barbuda. Andres is very familiar with the type of international fraud involving Odebrecht and Macri. If Trump's Argentina gambit and Panama City building had an connections to Odebrecht, Trump faced deeper legal trouble than anyone could have imagined. Keeping in mind that there were not many Latin American nations where Odebrecht had not been involved in bribery, the chances of a connection to Trump operations in Argentina, Panama, Uruguay, or the Dominican Republic were better than even.

At the 2011 grand opening of the hotel and office complex, Martinelli was present, along with Donald Trump, Donald Trump, Jr., and Ivanka Trump. Martinelli was positioned to provide Panamanian prosecutors detailed information on the Trump Organization's ties to Colombian drug cartels, Israeli and Ukrainian gangsters, and Russian mobsters who invested in condominiums in the Trump building in Panama City. Some of these same individuals invested in Trump condos in south Florida.

One of the most dangerous relationships between Trump and a Latin American country was that with Colombia. The nation elected Ivan Duque as its president in 2018. Duque's political mentor was former President Alvaro Uribe, who was linked to the infamous Medellin drug cartel. Uribe also happened to be a member of Trump's

Mar-a-Lago club in Palm Beach, Florida. It may not have been a slip of the tongue when Trump, speaking at a September 24, 2018 meeting at the United Nations on counter-narcotics, said of the Duque administration, "We look forward to partnering with his [Duque's] new administration to eradicate cocoa production in his country." While that was terrible news for chocolate lovers, it was a relief for Uribe's and Duque's friends in Colombia's coca-growing industry.

Many of the Trump Ocean Club Panama real estate transactions were carried out through Homes Real Estate and Investment Services of Panama City, headed by Alexandre Ventura Nogueira, a former Brazilian car salesman, who befriended Ivanka Trump. Nogueira also had links to the Valle del Norte drug cartel in Colombia and Uribe. On July 26, 2018, Uribe resigned his Colombian Senate seat to stand trial for making false statements and witness tampering.

Trump had not only been comfortable dealing with crime syndicates in Latin America, but also in New York. These included the Trincher gambling network and the Colombo, Lucchese, Genovese, and Gambino crime families. Trump would not be a very successful Godfather if he couldn't deal successfully with criminal syndicates that pervade the construction, real estate, and casino business. Robert Mueller's investigation of Trump and his family and associates led down many roads in several countries.

Trump became the Max Bialystock of American politics. Bialystock was the unscrupulous and washed-up Broadway showman in Mel Brooks's *The Producers*. Leo Bloom, the unwitting accountant who fell under Bialystock's con-artist trance, could have described Trump when he told a judge about his erstwhile business partner, "Not only is he a liar, and a cheat, and a scoundrel and a crook, who has taken money from little old ladies, but he's also talked people into doing things, especially me, that they would never, in a thousand years have dreamed of doing!" Mr. Trump, meet Max Bialystock, conman extraordinaire.

Following in the footsteps of the grifter-in-chief, Trump's Cabinet officials wasted no time in bilking the American people for all sorts of luxuries. U.S. ambassador to the United Nations Nikki Haley, while not lecturing other UN delegations like some schoolmarm, was buying motorized curtains for her Manhattan apartment, near UN Plaza. Price tag for the U.S. taxpayers: $52,701. Haley's brain-dense defenders pointed out that the curtain system was ordered in 2016. What they did not point out that Haley had a maid to open and close the curtains and the expenditure on such a needless contraption came as the State Department's budget had been slashed by a third, courtesy of his administration's America First goose steppers.

When it came to extravagant spending of the taxpayers' money, Ben Carson, Trump's Secretary of Housing and Urban Development, joined the hit parade of good-for-nothings. He spent $31,000 for a dining room set for his executive office. But, hey, it's on the taxpayers' dime, so what else would one expect from a physician who scammed unsuspecting consumers by endorsing a pyramid scheme of selling snake oil "nutrition supplements?" And, it was Carson who first relied on "fake news" to push his miracle drugs. His business manager was none other than Armstrong Williams, who had taken $240,000 from the administration of George W. Bush to propagandize for Dubya's "No Child Left Behind" scam in his radio and TV broadcasts and weekly syndicated columns in the Moonie-owned *Washington Times*.[49] Between Ditzy DeVos and her husband's Amway empire and Carson and his Mannatech company flim-flam, it was difficult to tell the difference between the Trump administration and a bunch of carnival barking grifters at a state fair.

Before he resigned in July 2018, Environmental Protection Agency administrator Scott Pruitt had become the chief grifter among an administration full of them. He spent $43,000 for a *Get Smart*-style secure telephone booth, what the fictional spy agency CONTROL called a "cone of silence." But Pruitt was even creepier than trying to emulate Agent 86, Maxwell Smart (Don Adams). Pruitt

---

[49] David Martosko, "Rising GOP star Ben Carson endorsed 'sham' nutrition supplement company – and employs 'business manager' linked to pay-for-play journalism scandal," *Daily Mail*, January 12, 2015.

sent an aide, on government time, to search for a used mattress from the Trump International Hotel. Perhaps, Pruitt had a fetish for bed bugs. Pruitt also used his government security detail to drive him around Washington to look for a moisturizing lotion found only at Ritz-Carlton hotels. Maybe Pruitt needed the cone of silence so no one at EPA would hear him moaning as he made maximum use of his Ritz-Carlton lotion.

Pruitt also used EPA resources to help arrange for his wife to open a Chick-fil-A fast food franchise and pick up his dry cleaning. Pruitt rang up $105,000 in first-class commercial flights plus another $58,000 in charter and military flights. They included a $16,217 December 2017 flight to Morocco, with an expensive overnight stay in Paris, to market American natural gas exports. And, everyone believed that was the domain of the Commerce or Energy Departments. There was also a first-class flight to Australia to conduct some "environmental" business, in addition to several first-class trips to Pruitt's home state of Oklahoma. Pruitt insisted that first-class domestic flights and a full security detail were necessary because some American citizens, upset with his hideous environmental policies, had, on previous occasions, given the Oklahoma crook a piece of their minds. Shudder to think that Americans had a right to tell off the grifting flim-flam man.

Pruitt felt it necessary to have the EPA purchase for his use "tactical pants" and "tactical shirts." He rented a lobbyist's Capitol Hill house for a mere $50 a night. It just so happened that the lobbyist, a shill for the energy industry, had pending business before the EPA. Pruitt also ran up his meal ticket at the White House mess, often taking his cronies there for lunch. For months, White House advisers complained to Trump about Pruitt's lack of ethics. Trump saw no problem with it until he faced a rebellion among Republicans in Congress.

Pruitt's actions on a visit to Rome also raised eyebrows in Washington. In 2017, Pruitt threw a huge dinner at a swank five-star restaurant in Rome with Cardinal George Pell, the Australian Roman Catholic Cardinal who later went on trial in Melbourne, Australia over charges of sexual abuse of young boys. The cost for the dinner was $240-a-head.

In 2017, Pruitt's fellow Oklahoma Republican, Senator Ralph Shortey, was charged by the Cleveland County District Attorney with molesting a 17-year old boy in a motel room in Moore, Oklahoma. State charges were dropped after Shortey was indicted on four federal sex trafficking and child pornography charges. In a plea deal, Shortey pleaded guilty to a single federal charge of sex trafficking on November 30, 2017.

Curiously, federal prosecutors agreed to drop charges against Shortey that were based on his smart phone containing child pornographic images. Pruitt served as Oklahoma's Attorney General during a time in which Shortey was known for an unusual degree of absenteeism in the state Senate, even though his district was very close to the capital of Oklahoma City. Shortey only seemed to show up to vote "yes" on bills that targeted gay and transgender people and supported gun rights. In

September 2018, Shortey was sentenced to fifteen years in prison.

Pruitt's replacement as acting administrator of the EPA was no gem. Andrew Wheeler had been caught "liking" a racist Facebook meme that depicted Barack and Michelle Obama staring at a banana. It was the sort of thing that passed for humor among the racist dregs of society who supported Trump.

Pruitt had an anti-environmental comrade-in-arms at the Interior Department. Interior Secretary Ryan Zinke was a walking and talking ethics violation in his own right.

In late 2017, the Interior Department's Inspector-General began investigating Zinke's use of charter flights to his Montana home. One of the flights was a June 2017 $12,475 taxpayer-funded charter flight from Las Vegas to Whitefish, Montana. Zinke, a former Navy SEAL, who stands accused of embellishing his military record, called the investigation of his use of charter flights "a little BS over travel."

Zinke grew up in Whitefish and he maintained a residence in the town of over 6000 people. Zinke claimed his private charter flight from Las Vegas was to attend a meeting of the Western Governors' Association, which met June 26-28, 2017. The keynote speaker was Frank Luntz, the right-wing pollster and focus group organizer. Zinke was also in Las Vegas to speak to the Vegas Golden Knights, the city's new National Hockey League team. The owner of the team, Bill Foley, was a major contributor to Zinke's campaign coffers.

In March 2017, Zinke flew in a chartered plane to the U.S. Virgin Islands. He followed up that charter flight trip with another, in May, to Alaska. The Interior Department refused to disclose the costs of the Virgin Islands and Alaska trips. In a bizarre comment, Zinke stated that he always made sure that "I am above the law." In the Trump administration, that was a very low bar.

Zinke retired from the Navy at the rank of Commander in 2008. Zinke failed to promote to Captain because of a June 1999 Officer's Fitness Report, which stated that Zinke was not recommended for promotion to Captain or being assigned to a command position. Zinke had been found guilty of billing the Navy for personal travel expenses for a trip from Washington state to Whitefish, a character flaw that followed Zinke into the position of Interior Secretary. Zinke claimed that his Navy visit to Montana was to conduct SEAL training, which turned out to be a lie. The Navy required Zinke to reimburse the service $211 for his personal trip.

Zinke, in his campaign ads, claimed to have led a force of more than 3,500 Special Operations personnel in Iraq in 2004. Retired Marine Corps Major General Michael S. Repass, Zinke's commanding officer in Iraq, called Zinke's claims a "stretch." It is noteworthy that Zinke's hometown of Whitefish was also a nexus for white supremacists and neo-Nazis. Whitefish and its former resident, Richard Spencer, the neo-Nazi who had, at the beginning of the Trump term, moved to Alexandria, Virginia.

After Spencer set up shop in Virginia to be closer to his friends in the Trump White House, including Trump special assistant Stephen Miller. the neo-Nazi website *Daily Stormer* announced that it was going to hold a march in Whitefish to protest against "Jews, Jewish businesses, and everyone who supports either." Although there were not many Jews living in Whitefish, about 100 in all, the Nazi website published photos of a Jewish realtor, along with her family, the pictures emblazoned with yellow "Jude" stars. These stars were required by Adolf Hitler's regime to be worn on the outer clothing of Jews living under the jackboots of the Third Reich.

The Trump administration was so jam-packed with crooks and grifters, a shiftless politico like Mike Pompeo, who succeeded Secretary of State Rex Tillerson after Trump fired him while on an official visit to Africa, looked like one of the "adults" in the room. Far from it, Pompeo was as crooked and dumb as his colleagues. Pompeo, a fundamentalist Christian, who rejected evolution and believed the Earth was a mere 6000 years old, felt more at home with fundie con artists like John Hagee, Pat Robertson, Paula White, Robert Jeffress, and Jerry Falwell, Jr. If brains were dynamite, the lot of them wouldn't have enough explosive power to blow their hats off their heads.

While he was Central Intelligence Agency director, Pompeo named his wife, Susan, as "honorary chair" of the Family Advisory Board, which gave her regular access to the above-secret seventh floor executive offices. Mrs. Pompeo possessed only a secret security clearance, but,

 nevertheless accompanied her husband on trips to the CIA training facility in Camp Peary, Virginia, also known as "The Farm."[50]

Pompeo, a member of the Kansas Tea Party, who managed to be elected to the U.S. House, was known as a pompous ass at the CIA and the State Department. In September 2018, the State Department, at Pompeo's direction, launched an Instagram account, in which the State Department became known as the "Department of Swagger."

Pompeo's photograph appeared along with those of William Shakespeare and General George S. Patton. Apparently, the word "swagger," which is the opposite of "tactfulness" -- what diplomacy is all about -- was first used by Shakespeare.[51]

---

[50] Jenna McLaughlin, "A family affair: Susan Pompeo's active role raising debate within the CIA," CNN, March 19, 2018.

[51] David Wade, "Why Is Trump's State Department Stealing Ideas from Old Spice Commercials?" *Politico*, September 13, 2018.

Apparently, Interior Secretary Ryan Zinke took "swagger" a bit too far. In a September 28, 2018 speech in Pittsburgh to the Consumer Energy Alliance, a pro-fracking lobbying group, Zinke bragged that the U.S. Navy could enforce a naval blockade of Russia. He said, "The United States has that ability, with our Navy, to make sure the sea lanes are open, and, if necessary, to blockade . . . to make sure that their [Russia's] energy does not go to market." Zinke also proffered the idea of a U.S. naval blockade of Iranian oil exports."[52]

Russian senator Alexei Pushkov immediately responded to Zinke's remarks by stating that a U.S. naval blockade of Russia would result in a Russian declaration of war against the United States, pursuant to international law. Pushkin said Zinke should try chewing gum, instead of saying something stupid.[53]

Zinke was not the only real-life version of Dr. Strangelove found in the Trump administration. On October 2, 2018, U.S. ambassador to NATO, former Senator Kay Bailey Hutchison (R-TX), told a news conference in Brussels that the United States reserved the right to "take out" a new Russian ground-launched cruise missile, citing a perceived violation of the 1987 Intermediate-Range Nuclear Forces Treaty. Considering how many treaties the Trump

---

[52] John Siciliano, "Ryan Zinke: Naval blockade is an option for dealing with Russia," *Washington Examiner*, September 28, 2018.

[53] Prensa Latina, "U.S. Naval Blockade Would Be Declaration of War, Russia Warns," September 30, 2018.

administration was tearing up, Hutchison's saber-rattling was hypocritical. The Russian Foreign Ministry replied that Hutchison was engaged in "aggressive rhetoric."[54]

  If they come, deny everything! Just act dumb. – Phil Silvers as Sgt. Bilko

Under Trump, the State Department was transformed into a three-ring circus, with Pompeo as the chief clown.

And what would be a Trump administration without a thoroughly creepy poster child for ethics violations, like Treasury Secretary Steve Mnuchin? This modern-day version of television's Master Sergeant Ernest G. Bilko, played by comedian Phil Silvers on *The Phil Silvers Show*, attempted to use a U.S. government jet to fly him and his newly-wed wife, Louise Linton, on their honeymoon to Europe. In August 2017, Mnuchin and wifey-poo bilked the taxpayers for a government-paid trip to Fort Knox, Kentucky, ostensibly to inspect America's gold reserves.

Considering the fact that Trump, a real life Goldfinger, is in the White House, it would not come as a surprise if no gold is left at Fort Knox. The actual reason for the Mnuchins' trip to Kentucky was to view the solar eclipse.

---

[54] Julian Borger, "US NATO envoy's threat to Russia: stop developing missile or we'll 'take it out,'" *The Guardian*, October 2, 2018.

Kentucky happened to be one of the best spots in the United States to view the eclipse.[55] Before Trump gave him the heave-ho, Secretary of Health and Human Services, Tom Price, tallied up $341,000 in charter flights, many for dubious reasons.

Trump's Transportation Secretary, Elaine Chao, the wife of Republican Senate Majority Leader Mitch McConnell, registered more than 290 hours of "private appointment" time during her first 14 months as Transportation Secretary. This was in addition to the time she was off for nights, weekends, paid vacation, and federal holidays. Much of the time off was on Friday afternoons and for long lunches.[56]

Another Cabinet-level grifter was Nikki Haley, the ambassador to the UN. Haley and her husband were found to have accepted a total of seven free luxury private flights between New York and Greenville, Charleston, and Aiken, South Carolina. The donors of the flights were three South Carolina businessmen. The day after an ethics complaint was filed with the State Department's Inspector-General about the flights, Haley abruptly announced her resignation as ambassador.

Another complete charlatan was Office of Management and Budget director Mick Mulvaney. Together with the

---

[55] Larry Noble, "Steve Mnuchin jet request only the start of White House ethics issues," *USA Today*, September 19, 2017.

[56] Tanya Snyder, Kathryn A. Wolfe, Beatrice Jin, "Where is Elaine Chao?" *Politico*, October 1, 2018.

porcine former GOP governor of Georgia, Sonny Perdue, the dastardly duo came up with a replacement for the Supplemental Nutrition Assistance Program (SNAP), commonly known as "food stamps," which provides food subsidies for the desperately poor. Instead of SNAP, which permits people to purchase fresh food in supermarkets, Mulvaney and Perdue, with Trump's blessing, advanced the Department of Agriculture's "America's Harvest Box." Instead of receiving a card used for food purchases, America's poor would receive a box containing high-sodium processed foods, including powdered milk, peanut butter, canned fruits and meats, and cereal.[57]

The Mulvaney-Perdue harvest box was one step away from providing Americans with nutritious high-energy ocean-derived plankton wafers called "Soylent Green" in a dystopian society that practiced mandatory euthanasia on the elderly. As we know from Detective Frank Thorn's (Charlton Heston) discovery at the end of the sci-fi classic, *Soylent Green*, "Soylent Green is people!"

The Trump administration turned into one big shakedown and extortion racket. Whether it was targeted sanctions on everyone from the judges and prosecutors of the International Criminal Court (ICC) in The Hague to the post-Robert Mugabe president of Zimbabwe, Emmerson

---

[57] Helena Bottemiller Evich, "Trump pitches plan to replace food stamps with food boxes," *Politico*, February 12, 2018.

Mnangagwa, the Trump administration threatened foreign individuals with U.S. visa bans and U.S. asset freezes.

Trade partners of the United States saw the Trump administration exact punishing tariffs, most of which hurt Americans, including farmers, factory workers, and importers and exporters. Of course, Trump was willing to negotiate with these countries, including Canada, the European Union, Mexico, China, Japan, and South Korea, but only on Trump's bombastic dictatorial terms.

And, of all people, who did Trump want in charge of U.S. commerce? None other than infamous Wall Street crook Wilbur Ross. In a display of billionaire hubris, Ross wore a pair of $500 customized Stubbs Wootton bedroom slippers, emblazoned with the Department of Commerce logo, to Trump's first address to Congress.[58] As marooned billionaire Thurston Howell III, played by Jim Backus, said on *Gilligan's Island*: "The Wizard of Wall Street strikes again!"

Ross had attested, on November 1, 2017, that he divested himself of all his assets in a business empire that included his vice chairmanship of the Bank of Cyprus. The bank was a favorite money laundering contrivance for Russian and Ukrainian oligarchs and Paul Manafort, Trump's later convicted 2016 campaign chairman. Ross, in typical fashion for a Trump administration, lied in his attestation.

---

[58] Jessica Estepa, "Commerce Secretary Wilbur Ross wore $500 slippers to Trump's address," *USA Today*, February 28, 2017.

He still owned upward of $50 million of stock in Invesco, the parent company of his W. L. Ross & Company.[59]

Ross's business partner in the Bank of Cyprus was one of Trump's real estate investors, Russian billionaire potash-fertilizer billionaire magnate, Dmitry Rybolovlev. Rybolovlev was a minority shareholder in the Cypriot bank.

Rybolovlev was also no stranger to gangster-like violence. In 1996, Evgeny Panteleymonov, Director of Neftekhimik, a firm partly owned by Rybolovlev, was shot and killed in his home. In May 1996, Rybolovlev was indicted and arrested for the contract killing of Panteleymonov. Rybolovlev was later released after the sole prosecution witness recanted his testimony.

It was no surprise that, according to Woodward's book *Fear*, that Trump said to Ross, "I don't trust you. I don't want you doing any more negotiations . . . You're past your prime."[60]

A March 8, 2017 letter addressed to President Trump from his tax attorneys, Morgan and Lewis of Washington, DC, and bearing the subject line "Transactions with Russian counterparties reported on your U.S. federal income tax returns" was intended to stifle Trump's critics iver his failure to fully release his tax returns, The letter stated that Trump only received Russian money from the 2013 Miss Universe pageant in Moscow and the $95 million sale

---

[59] Dan Alexander, "New Details About Wilbur Ross' Business Point To Pattern Of Grifting," *Forbes*, August 7, 2018.

[60] Woodward, *op. cit.*

of the 18-bedroom Maison de L'Amitié in Palm Beach, Florida to – voilá – Rybolovlev, Ross's business partner.

In terms of unconstitutional emoluments, cash payments to an American president by a foreign government, Trump was cleaning up through foreign government payments to his condominium properties in New York and hotel on Pennsylvania Avenue in Washington, DC.

Among the foreign governments that paid top dollar to the Trump International Hotel in Washington – located in the old U.S. Post Office building that was leased by the Trump Organization from the federal General Services Administration (GSA) -- were Turkey, Saudi Arabia, Kuwait, Azerbaijan, Cyprus, Bahrain, Philippines, Vietnam, and Georgia.

Trump and his daughter personally took in $3.9 million from the hotel in 2017. Nations renting units at Trump World Tower in Manhattan included Qatar, Saudi Arabia, India, and Afghanistan. It also became known that Jared Kushner and his ex-con father had both negotiated with Qatar a bailout by the wealthy emirate of the Kushner family's white elephant, a 41-story building at 666 Fifth Avenue in Manhattan that had been losing money. Until Qatar was finally extorted by the Trump administration to ante up

some bailout cash, Trump sided with the Saudis in calling Qatar a funding source for "Islamic" terrorism. In June 2017, Trump tweeted: "During my recent trip to the Middle East I stated that there can no longer be funding of Radical Ideology. Leaders pointed to Qatar – look!"

After Saudi King Salman and his powerful son and crown prince, Mohamed bin Salman, launched a brutal crackdown on rival princes, government ministers, and businessmen, a move that involved arbitrary arrest and detention, Trump expressed his support to the Saudi regime. He tweeted: "I have great confidence in King Salman and the Crown Prince of Saudi Arabia, they know exactly what they are doing . . . Some of those they are harshly treating have been 'milking' their country for years!" When it comes to milking a country dry, Trump and his family and cronies were without peers, including the Saudis.

On October 2, 2018, Washington, DC-based journalist and *Washington Post* columnist Jamal Khashoggi, a citizen of Saudi Arabia, resident of Virginia, and critic of the Saudi Crown Prince, walked into the Saudi consulate-general in Istanbul to obtain documentation requited for him to marry his Turkish fiancée. Khashoggi never emerged. A 15-member assassination team had arrived from Saudi Arabia aboard two private planes to kill Khashoggi. The team interrogated, tortured, and killed Khashoggi, followed by dismembering his body with a bone saw. It was like a scene right out of the 1997 film, *Donny Brasco*.

Trump, in remarks made at the White House on October 11, 2018, brushed off reports of Saudi involvement in the murder of Khashoggi, saying, "it's not our country. It's in Turkey, and it's [Khashoggi] not a citizen, as I understand it." It would not matter if Khashoggi was a citizen. Trump did not respond meaningfully after five members of the staff of the *Capital-Gazette* newspaper in Annapolis were gunned down by a crazed Trumper.

At a September 26, 2018 press conference in New York, Trump referred to King Salman as "King Solomon," displaying, once again, to his minions of fundie Christians that he had no concept of Biblical history. After all, this was the same buffoon who cited to a campaign crowd at Jerry Falwell's Liberty University in Virginia in January 2016 the biblical passage from "Two Corinthians 3:17," not, as it is known, Second Corinthians 3:17.

Falwell, who, like Pence and HUD grifter Ben Carson, believe the Earth is only 6000 years old, "baptized" Trump into the "prosperity gospel" cult. Although these Elmer Gantry types use Jesus of Nazareth in the same manner that GEICO uses a gecko lizard and Kia uses hamsters in their ad pitches, the prosperity gospel has absolutely nothing to do with the New Testament or Christianity. Mega-churches and their uber-wealthy pastors are as much a con game to Christianity as Trump buildings and Trump are to real estate.

Falwell showed his true colors in a Trumpian tweet sent on September 28, 2018:

"Conservatives & Christians need to stop electing 'nice guys'. They might make great Christian leaders but the US needs street fighters like @realDonaldTrump at every level of government b/c the liberal fascists Dems are playing for keeps & many Repub leaders are a bunch of wimps!"

In 2017, Falwell awarded Trump an honorary doctorate from Liberty University in Lynchburg, Virginia. It has as much academic value as a diploma from the defunct Trump University.

In 1981, Falwell's bloviating father, Jerry Falwell, Sr., criticized Ronald Reagan Supreme Court nominee Sandra Day O'Connor for her moderate views on abortion. Falwell said, "Every good Christian should be concerned" about O'Connor on the court. Senator Barry Goldwater, O'Connor's chief sponsor, replied, "Every good Christian should line up and kick Jerry Falwell's ass."

Falwell, Jr. was not the only snake oil preacher to come to Trump's defense. After it was revealed that Michael Cohen, Trump's lawyer and "fix it man" had recorded their conversation over hush money payments to porn actress Stormy Daniels, Baptist "Reverend" Robert Jeffress leaped to Trump's defense. Jeffress, who runs a Dallas megachurch, said that Trump was no worse than Ronald Reagan, who he called a "known womanizer."[61]

Jeffress and Falwell, Jr. were what passed for evangelical Christian leaders and they and others of their ilk were often invited to Trump events at the White House. Reagan,

---

[61] Samantha J. Gross, "Defending Donald Trump, First Baptist's Robert Jeffress compares him to 'known womanizer' Ronald Reagan," *Dallas News*, July 21, 2018.

who never entered the Oval Office without a suit jacket, would have been infuriated to have been compared to a shiftless bounder like Trump.

Using a global intertwined network of offshore shell corporations, domestic limited liability corporations, secret banks accounts, corrupt attorneys, and laundered money from international oligarchs and gangsters, Donald Trump was not only the President of the United States and commander-in-chief of the U.S. armed forces, but also a Mafiosi deep state chieftain.

Trump and his surrogates often complained about an amorphous U.S. "deep state," composed of the Federal Bureau of Investigation, the Central Intelligence Agency, the Department of Justice, and other departments and agencies, trying to undermine and overthrow the Trump administration. However, it was Trump's mafia deep state -- which resembled SPECTRE (SPecial Executive for Counterintelligence, Terrorism, Revenge and Extortion), the global criminal organization created by famed spy novelist Ian Fleming as the arch-enemy of British 007 secret agent, James Bond -- that posed an actual threat to America's democracy.

There were even actual parallels between Trump's real deep state and Bond's SPECTRE. The data research firm, Cambridge Analytica, based in London with a subsidiary in the United States -- once overseen by Trump's campaign strategist Steve Bannon -- had a close relationship with an engineer who once used the name Dr. Aleksandr (Alex) Spectre. Originally known as Aleksandr Kogan, he changed his last name to Spectre after moving in 2015 from Cambridge University in the United Kingdom to Singapore. And the similarities between Trump's deep state and SPECTRE do not end with Cambridge Analytica. A malicious program with Eurasian Mafia origins, which may have been used by Trump-linked computer hackers to break down the security of "secure" computer applications at the Democratic National Committee and personal email accounts of Trump political opponents, bore the name "Spectre."

Just like the fictional SPECTRE, Trump's real-life version of the criminal organization engaged in rather exotic murders of "problem" individuals. A Cambridge Analytica whistleblower named Christopher Wylie revealed that his former firm hired the Israeli intelligence firm Black Cube to hack the emails and medical records of Nigerian presidential candidate Muhammadu Buhari. The firm also conducted a psychographic voter micro-targeting campaign in Kenya's presidential election. Wylie said his predecessor at Cambridge Analytica died in a Kenyan hotel room, likely from poisoning, after a joint operation conducted with the Israeli firm Black Cube "went sour." Black Cube, which employed many ex-Mossad officers, was the same firm hired by disgraced Hollywood producer

Harvey Weinstein to dig up dirt on women who accused him of sexual assault.[62]

Various reports revealed that four Israeli companies associated with ex-members of Mossad, Shin Bet, and Unit 8200 -- Israel's signals intelligence and cyber-espionage agency -- assisted Cambridge Analytica in its "election engineering" operations. The firms were, in addition to Black Cube, PSY-Group, Wikistrat, and WhiteKnight. Joel Zamel, the co-founder of the latter three firms, served as an intelligence adviser to Abu Dhabi Crown Prince Mohammed bin Zayed al-Nahayan, who was also the major patron of Erik Prince's R2 and its cadres of Colombian, Chilean, Salvadoran, and South African mercenaries fighting in Yemen's civil war.

In a typical intelligence front fold-up operation, Cambridge Analytica, which employed Kogan/"Spectre" in its operation to mine data from Facebook, declared bankruptcy. PSY-Group later closed up its offices in Cyprus and Tel Aviv and transferred its operations to WhiteKnight, which was reportedly based in "parts unknown" (a hat tip to the late Anthony Bourdain and his TV show of the same name, who the author, occasionally, saw catching a smoke outside of Les Halles, his former restaurant on Pennsylvania Avenue in Washington, DC) in the Philippines and Caribbean.

---

[62] Haaretz and Reuters, "Cambridge Analytica Whistleblower Claims Israeli Firm Black Cube Was Hired to Hack African Election," *Haaretz*, March 27, 2018.

Others in the Trump campaign orbit began selling their "election manipulation" services abroad. Bannon traveled to Europe to help establish a "Fourth Reich International" in Brussels called "The Movement." This was aptly named, since this organization – a "bowel movement" -- was nothing more than an attempt by the far right in Europe to shit all over Europe's post-World War II democratic traditions.

Bannon was also working closely with Brazilian far-right and neo-Nazi presidential candidate Jair Bolsonaro. Bannon's operations in Brazil were coordinated with Bolsonaro's son, Brazilian congressman Eduardo Bolsonaro. Eduardo Bolsonaro revealed that Bannon provided assistance on the use of Internet-based social media for hyper-targeting and analyzing and interpreting polling and other data.[63]

Bolsonaro was nicknamed the "Tropical Trump." The reason was grotesquely obvious. Bolsonaro said that he, as president of Brazil, would take away the lands of Brazil's indigenous tribes and hand them over to private businessmen for exploitation. Bolsonaro also stated that "not one centimeter will be demarcated for indigenous reserves" and that if a "if a few innocent people die, that's alright." Bolsonaro called Afro-Brazilians "obese and lazy." More than half of all Brazilians were of African lineage. Bolsonaro also called refugees from Haiti, Africa, and the Middle East the "scum of humanity."

---

[63] Telesur, "Brazil: Steve Bannon to Advise Bolsonaro Presidential Campaign," August 15, 2018.

After Bolsonaro's election, John Bolton announced plans to meet the neo-Nazi president-elect in Rio de Janeiro.

Trump's former 2016 campaign manager, Corey Lewandowski, also cashed in. Avenue Strategies Global (ASG) – co-founded by Lewandowski and Barry Bennett, manager of Housing and Urban Development Secretary Ben Carson's 2016 presidential run – began selling political advice abroad. ASG, which was situated on a corner across from the White House, signed a lucrative contract with former Ukrainian prime minister Yulia Tymoshenko. It was obvious that Avenue Strategies was helping Tymosheno position herself for a future presidential run in Ukraine. And it was also quite convenient that ASG, from which Lewandowski later departed, was close, both geographically and politically, to the offices of Trump administration key officials, including National Security Adviser John Bolton.

Lewandowski became associated with another political advice consultancy, Turnberry Solutions, LLC of Washington, DC. Perhaps not coincidentally, Trump Turnberry was the name of Trump's Scottish golf resort. Yet another Lewandowski-linked firm, Washington East West Political Strategies LLC, which dissolved in 2017, advised political candidates in Albania and Kosovo and others in the Middle East, Canada, and Central America.

Erik Prince was under the microscope of several intelligence and law enforcement agencies around the world. With Trump in the White House, Prince confidently unveiled a start-up in Malta, Blackwater Ammunition. Some of Prince's militarized crop-dusting Thrush aircraft were also sighted in Malta. The parent company of Blackwater Ammunition was PBM Ltd. standing for Precision Ballistic Manufacturing. Blackwater Ammunition used the familiar bear claw logo used by the former Blackwater mercenary firm and its various offshoots.

What may have attracted Prince to Malta, other than its proximity to war zones in Libya and the trans-Sahel region, is that the island is the historical home of the Catholic order, the Knights of Malta. Prince and Rudolph Giuliani were both members of the Knights of Malta, which were expelled from Malta by Napoleon's army in 1798. The Sovereign Military Order of Malta relocated to Rome, where it enjoyed diplomatic privileges, including relations with 107 countries and the right to issue postage stamps. Prince was also a member of the Opus Dei, the far-right Catholic order, which, as Dan Brown fictionalized in *The DaVinci Code*, was known for being brutally aggressive toward its enemies.

Paid killers, in the employ of oligarchs who wanted to keep secret their plot to control the White House, may have very well been used to "eliminate" witnesses to computer hacking by Trump's mafia. These included Democratic National Committee staffer Seth Rich, gunned down on a Washington street on July 10, 2016, and Peter W. Smith, the Republican opposition research kingpin and Chicago investment banker who worked with a Russian hacker groups to obtain Hillary Clinton's emails. On May 14, 2017, nine days after revealing to *The Wall Street Journal* his contacts with the Russian hackers, Smith was found dead in a Rochester, Minnesota hotel room with a bag over his head that was attached to a helium tank. Authorities ruled Smith's death a suicide from asphyxiation.[64]

Trump's support network of Eurasian oligarchs possessed all of the assets that were available to Bond's nemesis. Just like SPECTRE, these oligarchs had at their disposal, in addition to paid assassins, 140-meter-long yachts with helicopter landing pads; private passenger jets; and estates in exotic locales like Seychelles, the "Emerald Coast" of Sardinia; Gstaad, Switzerland; the mountaintop village of Carsko Selo, Montenegro; the French Riviera; and the Greek island of Skorpios, once the domain of Greek shipping magnate Aristotle Onassis and his wife, Jacqueline Kennedy Onassis. These Eurasian mobster billionaires could practically buy anything they want, including elections, prime ministers, and, in the case of Trump, a President of the United States and the White House.

During the week prior to the November 2016 election, the luxurious Airbus A319 belonging to Russian fertilizer magnate Dmitry Rybolovlev was spotted on tarmacs near Trump's personal Boeing 757 at Charlotte's Douglas and Las Vegas's McCarran International Airports. Trump, who claimed he never met Rybolovlev, sold the Russian oligarch an oceanfront mansion in Palm Beach, Florida in 2008 for $100 million.

---

[64] Shane Harris and Reid J. Epstein, "Details Emerge in Suicide of GOP Activist Who Sought Hillary Clinton Emails, " *The Wall Street Journal*, July 14, 2017.

In many cases, the entities that have added to Trump's coffers by laundering money through his real estate enterprises, possess names that rival Ian Fleming's imagination. Investing in Trump's Las Vegas condominium tower is an entity called the "Black Tulip Organization."

Entities involved with Trump's indicted former National Security Adviser Michael Flynn included "GreenZone Systems" and "White Canvas Group." Eurasian Mafia firms involved with investors in Trump Tower condos in Manhattan include "Red and White Holdings Limited" and White Rock Partners & Company. Interestingly, an operation linked to the Kushner family's business operations was "White Rock Properties LLC." Other Kushner-linked firms included "White Garden Consultant Corporation" and "Black Elk Energy LLC."

The Trump Organization ran a business called "White Course LLC." A company connected to the Paul Manafort-Richard Gates business world was called "Yellow7, Inc." Another firm linked to the Trump presidential campaign is "Black Horse Resources LLC." And then there was the Israeli Mossad security firm "Black Cube" that worked with election data manipulators at Cambridge Analytica and its British parent firm, SCL Group.

In this version of Harold Arlen's and Yip Harburg's "Over the Rainbow" you have: ♫♫Somewhere over the rainbow . . . Way up high ♫♫ And the nightmare you dream of sure ain't no lullaby ♫♫

There were no pots of gold lying at the end of Trump's Mafia "rainbow," however, there was a multitude of secret bank accounts ranging from the Isle of Man to the Cook Islands.

Hashtag #TFA (Twenty-fifth Amendment)

When the history is written about the Trump administration and all the movies and documentaries about one of the most-shameful episodes in American history are produced, Donald Trump's behavior will be likened to Lieutenant Commander Philip Francis Queeg, the fictional commanding officer of the equally-fictional U.S. Navy minesweeper, the *USS Caine*. A classic novel, *The Caine Mutiny*, was set by writer Herman Wouk in the Pacific during World War II.

The 1954 motion picture, with the same title, starred Humphrey Bogart as Queeg, a mentally unstable ship captain who was more interested in discovering the identity of the culprit behind some missing strawberries in the officer's mess than in prosecuting the war against Japan and protecting his ship and crew.

After two of Queeg's officers relieve him of command of the ship for ignoring the dangers of an approaching typhoon, a Navy court-martial, convened in San Francisco, tried the two officers. During the unforgettable court-martial scene, Queeg demonstrates that he suffers from a paranoia disorder. The officers are acquitted after Queeg has a mental breakdown on the witness stand. But, *The Caine Mutiny* was fiction, after all. It could never actually occur higher in the military chain-of-command, especially all the way up to the Commander-in-Chief's level. Could it?

As September 2018 reached its second week, the primary talk of Washington and the nation was the identity of the anonymous high-level White House official who penned an op-ed piece in *The New York Times* castigating Trump's mental fitness for his office.

Just like Queeg aboard the Caine, Trump began lashing out at real and imagined enemies within the White House. He wanted Attorney General Sessions to launch a major investigation into the identity of the *Times* article, claiming that U.S. national security was at stake. Trump showed that he was more dangerous and delusional as Richard Nixon during his final days in office in 1974. Like Queeg and his quest for the wardroom's strawberry thief, Trump saw enemies in the shadows and recesses in every White House and Cabinet office. To Trump, the "Deep State" was out to get him.

The Washington Post ran a fascinating piece on September 10, 2018, just after some shocking segments about life inside the Trump administration, culled from Bob Woodward's tell-all book, *Fear: Trump in the White House*, were highlighted in the media.

The *Post* story revealed that the authors of the 25th Amendment of the Constitution, which lays out the procedure for relieving a president of his office in the event of physical or mental incapacitation, came from the scene in *The Caine Mutiny*, when the ship's executive officer relieves Queeg of his command. The dialogue was:

"Captain, I'm sorry, but you're a sick man. I'm relieving you as captain of this ship under Article 184."[65]
The 25th Amendment became the executive branch's version of Article 1874 of U.S. Navy Regulations. Although the application of the 25th Amendment passed a higher hurdle than what it takes to relieve a Navy commanding officer of his duties, the gist is the same.

Article 184 states: "Unusual Circumstances. It is conceivable that most unusual and extraordinary circumstances may arise in which the relief from duty of a commanding officer by a subordinate becomes necessary, either by placing him under arrest or on the sick list; but such action shall never be taken without the approval of the Navy Department or other appropriate higher authority, except when reference to such higher authority is undoubtedly impractical because of the delay involved or other clearly obvious reason. Such reference must set forth all facts in the case and the reason for the recommendation, with the particular regard to the degree of urgency involved."

In the case of the 25th Amendment, a majority of Cabinet officers and the Vice President must approve relieving the president of his duties, the decision only being permitted to stand with the approval of two-thirds of both houses of Congress.

---

[65] Meagan Flynn, "How 'The Caine Mutiny' influenced the debate over the 25th Amendment," *The Washington Post*, September 10, 2018.

Trump's mental instability became so apparent at the outset of his administration that Omarosa revealed that staffers would respond in Twitter messages with the hashtag of #TFA. TFA stood for Twenty-fifth Amendment.

In September 2018, *The New York Times*, in a report having dubious underpinnings, revealed that Deputy Attorney General Rod Rosenstein, after Trump's firing of FBI director Comey in May 2017, suggested, either in jest or in all seriousness, wearing a wire into the White House to capture on tape Trump's unfitness for office. Rosenstein denied the charge. Some observers believed that the story was proffered to the *Times* by anti-Rosenstein members of the Trump White House to justify Trump's sacking of Rosenstein, Attorney General Sessions, and ultimately special counsel Mueller. Another part of the *Times* story was that Rosenstein was in discussions with Sessions and then-Homeland Security Secretary John Kelly about canvassing the Cabinet to gather a majority to invoke the 25th Amendment. With all the other references to the "TFA," that part of the story may have had some substance.

In Trump Twitterdom, the press became known as the "Fake News Media." On July 31, 2018, Trump tweeted, "The Fake News Media is going CRAZY! They are totally unhinged and, in many ways, after witnessing the damage they do to so many innocent and decent people, I enjoy watching." It would take the combined talents to Drs. Sigmund Freud, Carl Jung, and B. F. Skinner to psychoanalyze that and other bizarre Trump tweets.

No wonder members of Trump's White House staff considered trying to invoke the 25th Amendment of the U.S. Constitution.

Dr. Bandy Lee, a psychiatry professor at the Yale University School of Medicine, revealed that in 2017, she was in discussions with White House staffers about Trump's mental "unraveling."

In 2017, Lee authored a book titled, *The Dangerous Case of Donald Trump: 27 Psychiatrists and Mental Health Experts Assess a President*. In an interview, Lee told Salon: "Donald Trump has shown a number of symptoms which are now quite obvious to even an untrained person. He is impulsive. He is reckless. He has shown a lack of empathy and a lack of concern about consequences. His grip on reality is loose. I suspect he is unable to tolerate reality for what it is. So, Trump has to make himself into a person who is infallible and an expert on everything."

Lee added, "Therefore, when reality does not comport with his emotional needs, he has to fabricate his own version of reality. Trump has also shown a tendency of needing to present himself as being strong and powerful. He is constantly preoccupied with his self-image, he is unable to tolerate criticism and he lashes out when there is a hint of anyone being against him or challenging his authority."[66]

---

[66] Chauncey Devega, "Psychiatrist Bandy Lee: Trump is getting worse; 'I suspect he is unable to tolerate reality,'" Salon, September 21, 2018.

Another Trump favorite was to constantly reject "Collusion." With reference to his campaign's strong links to Russian-Ukrainian-other Eastern European organized criminal syndicates and troll farms of social media manipulators, Trump had a pat response: "Collusion is not a crime, but that doesn't matter because there was no Collision (except by Crooked Hillary and the Democrats!" To parse Trump's tweet, he was alleging that Hillary Clinton, his Democratic opponent in 2016, colluded with the Russians to ensure her own defeat and Trump's victory. Calling Drs. Freud, Jung, and Skinner!

In late September 2018, *The New York Times* reported that Deputy Attorney General Rosenstein had, either in a fit of pique or in jest, suggested wearing a wire into the White House to gain audio evidence that could be used to convince the Cabinet to invoke the 25th Amendment. Rosenstein had just been thrust into the toxic political fray in Main Justice after Trump unceremoniously fired Comey as FBI director. Trump immediately began floating on Fox News and other right-wing outlets insinuations that Rosenstein's days as Deputy Attorney General were numbered.[67]

The right-wing spin machine of Fox and right-wing xenophobic talk radio began demanding Trump rid his

---

[67] Adam Goldman and Michael S. Schmidt, "Rod Rosenstein Suggested Secretly Recording Trump and Discussed 25th Amendment," *The New York Times*, September 21, 2018.

administration of the "deep state," a phantom assortment of anti-Trump forces. To hear Trump supporters constantly repeat the phrase "deep state," as it was associated with career civil servants, was to hear Dorothy and her three friends, the Scarecrow, Tin Man, and Cowardly Lion, repeat "lions, and tigers, and bears. oh my," as they traversed the deep and dark forest of Oz.

One person who had the modus operandi and capability to dangle dubious stories to the mainstream media was the White House deputy chief of staff for communications, Bill Shine. Shine had been the president of Fox News. He was never a working journalist, but a TV ratings monger. In 2001, during the news cycle dealing with the disappearance of DC intern Chandra Levy, the girlfriend of Democratic Congressman Gary Condit, Shine hired two psychics who claimed they knew where to find the body of Levy. In May 2017, Shine was fired by Fox News over his role in covering up sexual harassment charges leveled against Fox chairman Roger Ailes and host Bill O'Reilly. Trump, always eager to bring in the worst misogynistic talent into the White House, appointed Shine to his White House position in July 2018.

Shine was a master of dissembling the facts surrounding legitimate news story to fit the right-wing spin machine. Shine's wife, Darla Shine, an individual who had posted racist insults in social media, which included defending the use of the word "nigger."[68]

---

[68] Caleb Ecarma, "Bill Shine's Wife Darla Complained She Couldn't Use N-Word and Spread Conspiracy Theories About 'Blacks,'" Mediaite, July 6, 2018.

Trump's affectation for Fox News, which he watched from the White House, his golf clubs, and Air Force One, was reminiscent of the movie character Chance the Gardener, played by Peter Sellers, in the 1979 film, *Being There*.

Chance lives in a Washington, DC townhouse of a wealthy old man, only tending the garden and never venturing from the residence. After the old man dies, Chance wanders the streets, homeless, and is eventually discovered by Ben Rand (played by Melvyn Douglas), a wealthy confidante of the president of the United States.

Rand introduces Chance to DC's elite as "Chauncey Gardiner," an expert on just about any subject. Chauncey Gardiner even develops a close bond with the Soviet ambassador. Donald Trump is nothing more than a vile version of Chauncey Gardiner, someone who rarely leaves his own reality and watches too much Fox News. In fact, Trump relies on advice from Hannity, O'Reilly, and Lou Dobbs, the latter advertised as a Fox Business News Wall Street "expert."

Trump's oral and digital outbursts indicated the president of the United States was mentally off his rocker. It was more than likely that the authors of the 25th Amendment, who drafted the constitutional alteration in 1967, contemplated that the American electorate would never be foolish enough to vote for someone as bananas as Trump. They did envisage a president who might suffer from severe depression or even suicidal thoughts. But, a raving lunatic?

The world may never know Trump's true medical and psychiatric history. On February 3, 2017, after Trump was only in office for a few weeks, Trump's personal bodyguard, Keith Schiller; Trump's lawyer, Alan Garten; and a third unknown man, stormed into the Manhattan office of Trump's personal physician, Dr. Harold Bornstein. Later, Bornstein revealed that the office raid left him feeling "raped, frightened and sad."[69]

Dr. Bornstein's mistreatment by Trump brought back a certain scene in the sci-fi movie *Independence Day*.  President Thomas J. Whitmore, played by actor Bill Pullman, is spirited to Nevada's Area 51 after aliens lay waste to Washington, DC. Whitmore is the introduced to Dr. Brackish Okun, a rather weird scientist, played by Brent Spiner. Dr. Okun has been experimenting for decades on captured alien bodies and their crashed spacecraft. Bornstein and Okun represent two rather whacky lookalikes trying to please a president during trying times. Area 51 had less secrets in *Independence Day* than did Trump's medical record in real life. Ponder that for a second.

---

[69] Katie Rogers and Lawrence K. Altman, MD, "Trump's Former Doctor Says Office Was Raided and Files Seized," *The New York Times*, May 1, 2018.

When Speaker of the House John McCormack and Senate President (and Vice President) Hubert Humphrey signed the 25th Amendment in 1967, after it was ratified by 47 states, and sent it to President Lyndon Johnson for certification, it is doubtful that any of the congressional sponsors could have predicted a Trump.

Paraphrasing Republican Senator Howard Baker's signature question during the Senate Watergate hearings, "When did the President go nuts and when did his staff know it?"

Trump's 2 Million Minutes of Hate

The political party faithful in George Orwell's 1984 fictional state of Oceania are required to collectively watch a film that denounces the enemies of Big Brother. At the end of the film, the crowd erupts into two minutes of intense rage at Big Brother's enemies, most notably Emmanuel Goldstein, with some throwing things at the telescreen. The "two minutes hate" in Donald Trump's America equates to some 2 million minutes of hate, considering that for Trump's initial four-year term in office, his most ardent loyalists, encouraged by Trump's hateful comments and tweets, felt empowered to carry out mindless acts of hatred upon others.

Norman Lear, the creator of the Archie Bunker character in the television comedy, "All in the Family," likened Bunker to Trump. During the 2016 campaign, Lear said of Trump,

"He is Archie Bunker . . . I think of Donald Trump as the middle finger of the American right hand. Why is this happening? Whether you're Republican or a Democrat, can we all seriously agree this is bad for America?"

Rob Reiner, who played Bunker's long-haired and liberally-inclined son-in-law on "All in the Family," said on Stephen

Colbert's show on CBS, "We've got Archie in the White House."[70]

With all due deference to Lear and Reiner, Archie, who lived in Queens, Trump's home borough, was certainly bigoted but not mean-spirited to his very core. When it came down to brass tacks, Archie, a product of the Depression and World War II era, would lend a helping hand to anyone truly in need. Trump, on the other hand, would piss on somebody on fire and then take credit for helping the victim.

Trump was fond of re-tweeting racist and factually untrue tweets sent by Britain First leader Jayda Fransen. Britain First is tied to British neo-Nazis and white supremacists. To Trump, transatlantic neo-Nazis were "fine people on both sides."

The much-anticipated constitutional crisis many feared would come about under Trump's bombastic style of leadership occurred a mere week into his administration. Trump's Executive Order banning visitors, including U.S. permanent resident "green card" holders and those with valid U.S. visas, was one of the most poorly planned and implemented White House regulation in recent memory.

Trump and his henchmen immediately began to denounce U.S. judges who issued stays on executing Trump's order.

---

[70] John Bowden, "Rob Reiner on Trump: We have Archie Bunker in the White House," *The Hill*, August 4, 2018.

The first judge to issue a stay on Trump's visa ban was Ann Donnelly, a former New York state prosecutor. She was nominated by Barack Obama to the U.S. District Court for the Eastern District of New York in Brooklyn. A native of Michigan and a graduate of Ohio State's Moritz College of Law, nothing suggested that Donnelly was a rank-and-file Democrat, something alleged by Trump's spokespeople and media propagandists. In fact, the Republican Senate voted in 2015 to confirm Donnelly in a 95-2 vote.

When a number of New York City area politicians showed up at JFK International Airport with a copy of Judge Donnelly's order and demanded the release of detainees, clueless Customs and Border Protection (CBP) agents feigned ignorance because their ultimate boss, Secretary of Homeland Security John Kelly, had not been briefed beforehand about Trump's cockamamie and ill-prepared executive order.

The next judge to issue a temporary restraining order was Leonie Brinkema, a no-nonsense judge sitting on the federal bench of the national security, the so-called "Rocket docket" of the U.S. District Court for the Eastern District of Virginia in Alexandria. So named because it often sided with the government in national security-related cases, it would normally be the last court where a national security matter would be ruled against. However, Brinkema, who sentenced the "20th hijacker" Zacarias Moussaoui to life imprisonment in the Colorado "Supermax" prison, stayed Trump's executive order and ruled that the removal and deportation of green card holders from Dulles International Airport was suspended for seven days.

Brinkema also ordered that lawyers be given access to those being detained at Dulles. That order was immediately ignored when lawyers and three U.S. House members, Virginia Representatives Don Beyer and Gerry Connolly, and Maryland Representative Jamie Raskin, as well as New Jersey Senator Cory Booker, were denied access to the detained passengers at the airport by members of the Metropolitan Washington Airports Authority (MWAA) police.

The airport cops were answerable not to the DHS or CPB but to the independent MWAA commission, members of which are appointed by the governors of Maryland and Virginia and the mayor of the District of Columbia, with only three appointed by the president. The fact that glorified airport rent-a-cops disregarded a federal court order and those of three members of the House and one U.S. senator was a definite troubling bellwether of things to come.

The third judge to issue a stay on the White House order was Thomas Zilly of the U.S. District Court for the Western District of Washington in Seattle. Zilly, who ordered all deportations be halted by Trump, was nominated by President Ronald Reagan. So much for the brain-dead meme by Trump supporters that the order was nullified by "Democrat judges," a major "alternative fact" in Zilly's case.

The fourth and fifth judges who temporarily stayed Trump's deportation order were U.S. magistrate judge Judith Dein and District Court judge Allison Burroughs, both of the U.S. District Court for the District of Massachusetts in Boston. Dein was nominated by Bill

Clinton and Burroughs by Obama. Both were confirmed by Republican-controlled Senates, Dein in 2000 and Burroughs in 2014.

Comments began to appear on a number of dubious pro-Trump websites that called for unspecified "action" against the five judges.

U.S. District Judge for the Central District of California Dolly Gee became the sixth federal judge to block Trump's executive order on deportations. She ordered the immediate return to the United States of Iranian national Ali Vayeghan, a U.S. visa holder, who was deported from Los Angeles to Dubai. Vayeghan was en route to see his son, a U.S. citizen, in Indiana. Gee ruled that Trump's immigration ban violated the Establishment Clause of the First Amendment of the Constitution.

Trump's order also resulted in acting Attorney General of the United States Sally Yates proclaiming that the Justice Department would not defend Trump's order in court, as it was a violation of the Constitution and the Immigration and Nationality Act. Judge Gee was nominated by President Obama and she was unanimously confirmed by the Senate in December 2009. Yates was a non-partisan career Justice Department prosecutor. Trump ordered Yates fired, an act that many viewed as a repeat of the "Saturday Night Massacre" of October 1973, when President Richard Nixon fired his Attorney General and Deputy Attorney General for refusing Nixon's command to sack the Watergate special prosecutor.

In an utter display of vindictiveness and hatred, Trump decided to go after the security clearances of his critics.

On August 15, 2018, Donald Trump announced, via White House Press Secretary Sarah Huckabee Sanders, that he had revoked the security clearance of former CIA director John Brennan. The move came a month after Trump threatened to revoke the clearances of a list of former national security officials, including Brennan. After announcing the revocation of Brennan's clearance, Sanders announced that the clearances of other former national security and law enforcement officials were currently under review, with a possibility that they, too, could be revoked.

The list includes former Director of National Intelligence James Clapper, former CIA and National Security Agency director Michael Hayden, former national security adviser Susan Rice, former acting Attorney General Sally Yates, former FBI director James Comey, former FBI deputy director Andrew McCabe, former FBI counter-intelligence division chief Peter Strzok, former associate Attorney General Bruce Ohr, and former FBI lawyer Lisa Page. Comey, McCabe, and Strzok were fired from their FBI positions. Ohr continues to work at the Department of Justice as a member of the Senior Executive Service.

Former FBI officers believed that in revoking Brennan's clearance and threatening those of the others on the list, Trump was signaling to Justice Department special counsel Robert Mueller that the White House could sidetrack the investigation of Trump's and his associates' criminal activities by simply revoking the security clearances of, and, thus, access to classified information by Mueller and his team of prosecutors. Such a move would, under normal circumstances, result in obstruction of justice charges being drawn up in the House of Representatives and sent to the Senate for an impeachment trial. Sarah Huckabee Sanders, in answer to a question at a press briefing about whether others, in addition to those she named, might also face revocation of their clearances, she replied, "we would certainly take a look and review those as well."

Sanders had all the charm of Annie Wilkes (played by Kathy Bates), the deranged fan of novelist Paul Sheldon, played by James Caan, in the movie *Misery*. Sanders missed a chance to echo Wilkes in defense of Trump's use of the pejorative "rocket man" to describe North Korean leader Kim Jong Un. Wilkes tells a bed-ridden Sheldon in *Misery*: "And there was Rocketman, trying to get out, and here comes the cliff, and just before the car went off the cliff, he jumped free! And all the kids cheered! But I didn't cheer. I stood right up and started shouting. This isn't what happened last week! Have you all got amnesia? They just cheated us! This isn't fair! He didn't get out of the cock-a-doodie car!" There is just something about Sarah Huckabee Sanders that screams out "cock-a-doodie."

The drawing up by Trump of a list of political enemies to be dealt with by government action was reminiscent of Richard Nixon's infamous enemy's list. Those on Nixon's enemies list were to be audited by the Internal Revenue Service. The list was prioritized, with those at the top to be audited first by the IRS.

Many Americans may have patted themselves on the back, albeit prematurely, when the United States elected its first African-American president in 2008. Yet, in eight years, some of Obama's white supporters, particularly in the rust belt states, decided to vote for Trump. What Trump instilled in his "base" of those bearing pent-up hatred for what they considered as "the others" – African-Americans, Hispanics, Muslims, Asian-Americans, and even Native Americans – was something that had reared its ugly head in the 1930s: America First, an ideology not born in the Jim Crow South, but in Nazi Germany.

Few white Americans could understand the world in which African-Americans and Hispanics awoke on the morning of November 9, 2016. It was something right out of Philip K. Dick's, *The Man in the High Castle*. It was a dystopian United States governed by Nazis, not wearing brown shorts and jack boots, but business suits and Gucci shoes. This Trumpian America was no less dangerous than that portrayed in *The Man in the High Castle* novel and its adaptation for television.

Trump curried favor with America's racists by personally attacking African-American icons, including Barack Obama, National Basketball Association (NBA) star LeBron James, and CNN anchor Don Lemon. On August 3, 2018, Trump tweeted: "Lebron James was just interviewed by the dumbest man on television, Don Lemon. He made Lebron look smart, which isn't easy to do. I like Mike!" "Mike" was a reference to basketball star Michael Jordan, who immediately rejected Trump's attack on James. On June 28, 2018, Trump tweeted that Representative Maxine Waters of California was: "an extraordinarily low IQ person."

During the 2018 mid-term election races, Trump's tweets suggested that two strong African-American Democratic candidates for governor were "pro-crime." It was a typical racist dog-whistle that hearkened back to the days of Police Commissioner Bull Connor in Alabama and Governor Lester Maddox of Georgia. Trump called Stacey Abrams, running for governor of Georgia, an "open border crime loving opponent." To Trump, Florida's gubernatorial candidate, Andrew Gillum, the mayor of Tallahassee, was a "a failed Socialist Mayor . . . who has allowed crime & many other problems to flourish in his city."

As usual, Trump was more full of shit than a Christmas goose. However, for too many law enforcement officers across the United States, Trump's racist messages had receptive ears. And death ensued.

There were countless cases of cops becoming judges, juries, and executioners in meting out punishment to people of color. In the case of Botham Shem Jean, a native of St. Lucia, who worked for PricewaterhouseCoopers in Dallas, Trump's America led to a death sentence. In September 2018, an off-duty white female cop said she "mistakenly' entered Jean's apartment instead of her own and shot to death Jean.

In a normal America, Jean's death would have elicited a response from the White House. Jean's mother, Allison Jean, was a former permanent secretary of the St. Lucia Department of Education, Innovation and Gender Relations. She was in New York, participating in the meetings that normally precede the annual General Assembly's plenary session. Jean's "murder by cop" sent shockwaves through the normally placid island of St. Lucia. St. Lucia's Prime Minister Allen Chastanet arrived in Dallas to investigate the circumstances of Jean's murder.

Not one official of the Trump administration was in Dallas to greet Chastanet and Trump mentioned Chastanet's fellow Caribbean prime minister, Ralph Gonsalves, the Prime Minister of St. Vincent and the Grenadines, summed up at the September 2018 UN General Assembly plenary meeting how Trump and his ilk were viewed by the rest of the world: "Craven demagogues, clothed in populist robes, have emerged to exploit economic hardship and fan the flames of division, hatred and isolation." Chastanet, who was in New York with Gonsalves and other Caribbean leaders, reminded the General Assembly, and, particularly the U.S. delegation, that, "we must be willing to challenge discrimination and exclusion if we endeavor to create an equal and just world for all."

It did not matter one bit that Chastanet had to help bury one of St. Lucia's citizens who was gunned down in Trump's resurgent racist America. His words and those of the other world leaders fell on the deaf ears of the U.S. delegation, headed by Trump's opportunistic "honorary white southern belle," Nikki Haley.[71] Trump made no effort to apologize to Chastanet for the incident, something that every one of Trump's predecessors would have done.

The death of Jean and the snubbing of Chastanet by Trump was followed by news that Alexander Nix, the former CEO of Cambridge Analytica, which was so key to Bannon's strategy on winning the 2016 election for Trump, was, himself, an avowed racist. In October 2018, the release of

---

[71] Haley, the former Republican Governor of South Carolina, is the daughter of Indian Sikh parents, who immigrated to the United States via Vancouver, Canada.

Nix's emails showed the world that the election manipulators who surrounded Bannon were rank racists. In October 2010, Nix, after unsuccessfully pitching his firm's election services to then-Barbados Labor Party (BLP) opposition leader Mia Mottley and BLP senator Lucille Moe, wrote the following about the BLP leaders: "They just niggers."[72] Mottley became prime minister in May 2018 and Moe was named information minister.

For the Caribbean region, Trump was a vile banana republic dictator, the likes of which they had seen before: in Haiti with the "Papa" and "Baby Doc" Duvaliers and Grenada with Eric Gairy.

In May 2018, members of the White House Press Corps noticed something unusual occurring on the North Lawn of the White House, just outside the press briefing room. A sink hole had appeared. And, it was growing larger by the day. There was a hope among some of the more religious folks viewing the growing chasm that Satan was calling home his disciple, Donald Trump. However, even incantations to the Prince of Darkness went unheeded. Trump did not go anywhere, except to his golf resorts in New Jersey, Florida, and northern Virginia. Apparently, hell

---

[72] Juliette Garside and Hilary Osborne, "Former Cambridge Analytica chief used N-word to describe Barbados PM," *The Guardian*, October 8, 2018.

had no time for the bastard and the sink hole at the White House stopped growing and was, eventually, filled in.

Trump's racist dog whistles to his minions were crystal clear. Unfortunately, not only racist civilians decided to physically attack people of color, but law enforcement officers weighed in by committing wanton acts of extrajudicial killings of African-Americans across the United States. No white person could really understand the living hell that people of color dealt with every time they got into their cars and drove to work, the store, school, or church. Would they be stopped by a cop in a "driving while black" moment? Would they or members of their families even return home that evening and not end up in a morgue, courtesy of some Trump-inspired trigger-happy cop?

Botham Jean's murder by cop became an international incident. Many others killed by cops – Jordan Edwards of Texas, Antwon Rose of Pennsylvania, Dewboy Lister of Texas, Daniel Hambrick of Tennessee, to name four out of hundreds -- received varying degrees of press attention, but all were horrific. In 2017 alone, of the 147 unarmed people killed by cops in America, 48 were black and 34 were Hispanic.[73] This chapter could go on to name all those murdered since Trump took his notorious escalator ride to the lobby of the Trump Tower on June 16, 2016, which was, to use a quote from Franklin Roosevelt, "a day that will live in infamy."

---

[73] policeviolencereport.org

There's a "fucking moron" in the Oval Office

Yes, folks, a "fucking moron" was sworn in as President of the United States on January 20, 2017. That date will rival the Japanese attack on Pearl Harbor as a "date which will live in infamy." Apologies to those who might be offended by the language, but they are not this writer's words, but those of Secretary of State Rex Tillerson after attending a Pentagon briefing at which Donald Trump had no clue what was being discussed.

Trump's stupidity at the Pentagon briefing was not the first nor the last time he would display his pathetic ignorance. When Trump would try to give an on-topic speech, only to veer off the subject into unimportant issues like television ratings and attacking show business celebrities, it is too bad that someone was not in a position to stop him and recite what comedian-actor Jim Downey, playing a school principal, tells Billy Madison (Adam Sandler) in the eponymous 1995 film.

Downey, emceeing a *Jeopardy*-style game show, tells the obnoxiously stupid Madison: "What you've just said is one of the most insanely idiotic things I have ever heard. At no point in your rambling, incoherent response were you even close to anything that could be considered a rational thought. Everyone in this room is now dumber for having listened to it. I award you no points, and may God have mercy on your soul." Billy Madison, incidentally, is a 27-

year old heir to a major hotel chain founded by his father. Sounds a bit familiar.

May Mike Pence, who believes he pinch hits for God, have mercy on Donald Trump's soul.

Authors who wrote insiders' accounts of the machinations within the Trump White House were vilified by Trump and his sycophantic supporters. The first to receive Trump's ire was Michael Wolff, who was given permission to just hand around the White House. In *Fire and Fury: Inside the Trump White House*, which was released in January 2018, Wolff wrote that "100 percent" of Trump's senior advisers and even family members questioned his fitness for the office of president. Wolff added that Trump acted "like a child." Trump's lawyers responded to Wolff's book by sending a cease and desist letter to Wolff and his publisher, Henry Holt & Company. The letter, as with all of the threats from Team Trump, was simply rejected as a frivolous attempt at censorship.

Next at bat was Secretary of State Rex Tillerson. When Trump selected Tillerson, the then-chief executive officer of ExxonMobil, as his Secretary of State nominee on December 13, 2016, the president-elect said his pick was one of the "truly great business leaders of the world."

The nice words between the two would not last long. On March 22, 2017, Tillerson began expressing his exasperation in his job, the most senior-level of the Cabinet. On a trip to Asia, Tillerson told a reporter for the right-wing *Independent Journal Review*, "I didn't want this job. I didn't seek this job . . . My wife told me I'm supposed to do this."[74]

Tillerson, who was America's chief diplomatic envoy to countries around the world, including those in Africa and Latin America-Caribbean, was not at all pleased with Trump's comments on August 27, 2017, about white supremacist and neo-Nazi demonstrators in Charlottesville, Virginia being "fine people." Tillerson brusquely told Fox News, "the president speaks for himself."

On October 1, 2017, Trump tweeted that Tillerson's negotiations with North Korea were a "waste of time." Three days later, on October 4, NBC News and the *New Yorker* reported that after a July 20, 2017, meeting at the Pentagon, attended by Tillerson, Secretary of Defense James Mattis, and other top officials, Tillerson called Trump a "fucking moron."

---

[74] Alana Abramson, "Secretary of State Rex Tillerson: 'I Didn't Want This Job,'" *Fortune*, March 22, 2017.

In an interview with *Forbes* magazine, published on October 10, 2017, Trump challenged Tillerson to take an IQ test. Trump's petulant quote was, "I think it's fake news, but if he did that, I guess we'll have to compare IQ tests. And I can tell you who is going to win." So, Trump was going to beat the man he called one of the "truly great business leaders of the world" to an IQ test duel. While Whereas Tillerson presided over one of the largest publicly-traded companies in the world, Trump, who led a privately-held company, with family members and cronies on his board of directors and no outside shareholders, thought of himself as a peer of Tillerson's. "Fucking moron" did not even begin to describe Trump. Tillerson's statement also proved journalist H. L. Mencken's prognostication in the July 26, 1920 *Baltimore Evening Sun* correct: that "the White House will be adorned by a downright moron."

"The White House will be adorned by a downright moron."

H. L. Mencken

On March 10, 2018, after Tillerson, the previous day, said the proper conditions for direct U.S. talks with North Korea had not been met, Trump announced direct negotiations with North Korea were beginning. To the embarrassment of U.S. foreign service personnel around the world, Trump humiliated the Secretary of State. Three days later, Trump fired Tillerson, along with Undersecretary for Public Diplomacy Steve Goldstein.

In a case of musical chairs on the deck of the American ship of state, Trump nominated his Central Intelligence Agency director, Mike Pompeo, a former Tea Party congressman from Kansas, to replace Tillerson. CIA careerist Gina Haspel was nominated to replace Pompeo at Langley, Virginia. Throughout American history, no Cabinet-level official had ever been so publicly humiliated as was Tillerson. Only a "fucking moron" could have acted so impulsively.

The next tell-all author to come in for Trump's idle threats was former top White House aide Omarosa Manigault Newman. In August 2018, the former "Apprentice" star released "Unhinged: An Insider's Account of the Trump White House." Almost immediately, the Trump for President campaign, which had transitioned from 2016 to 2020 mode, sued Manigault-Newman for violating a 2016 "non-disclosure agreement" (NDA) with the campaign. It was another idle threat from a bully whose entire business career was predicated on launching frivolous lawsuits against contractors, sub-contractors, and media critics. NDAs were virtually unheard of in previous administrations. However, no previous administration was as bumbling, inept, and as mean-spirited as Trump's.

Simon & Schuster, the publisher of Omarosa's book, rejected Trump's threat as a "hollow legal threat." Trump never realized that as president, he did not have the same swagger as President and CEO of the Trump Organization. A restraining order known as the U.S. Constitution prevented Trump from bullying and intimidating his critics.

Simon & Schuster, like Henry Holt & Company, told Trump's chief media litigator, Charles Harder, a Beverly Hills, California-based attorney for celebrities, to basically go pound sand. Harder had represented First Lady Melania Trump in a successful $2.9 million lawsuit against the United Kingdom's *Daily Mail*. While Trump may have been successful with that suit, it was the last time the press would be browbeaten by Trump and his legal muscle.

After Trump sent the First Lady to Texas to survey the situation with hundreds of children of asylum-seeking migrants from Latin America being separated from their parents – something that erupted in almost-universal condemnation of Trump and his policies – Mrs. Trump's airy disengagement from her husband's brutality became known to the world. Boarding a plane at Joint Base Andrews sporting a jacket that had the phrase "I Really Don't Care Do U?" on the back, Melania's Marie Antoinette-like demeanor resulted in immediate criticism. How could anyone with an ounce of empathy wear such a thing when visiting the scene of the forced separations of families. Adolf Hitler's mistress, Eva Braun, never made a known trip to a train depot or concentration camp where parents were forcibly separated from their children.

And what did Mrs. Trump's photo op with child detention center officials in Texas achieve for the benefit of the families rendered apart? Not a damned thing.

Ironically, it was Britain's *Daily Mail*, the paper sued by Melania in 2017, that first reported on the jacket incident.

Maybe Trump wanted his third wife to appear as some poised and cultured European. However, after the jacket incident, she was seen by many as a highfalutin mail-order East European bride, whose only interest in immigrating to the United States appeared to be "to make fuck with rich fat man to get green card and maybe U.S. passport for me, mama, and papa."

On September 5, 2018, just prior to the release of Woodward's book, *Fear, The New York Times* published on its op-ed page a column written by an anonymous high-level official in the Trump administration. In the column, titled, "I am Part of the Resistance Inside the Trump Administration," the official, clearly a doctrinaire Republican conservative, revealed the inner workings of a White House staff that had considered involving the 25th Amendment because of Trump's inability to carry out his presidential duties.

Some highlights of the column:

- "The dilemma — which he [Trump] does not fully grasp — is that many of the senior officials in his own administration are working diligently from within to frustrate parts of his agenda and his worst inclinations.

- "... we believe our first duty is to this country, and the president continues to act in a manner that is detrimental to the health of our republic."
- "The root of the problem is the president's amorality. Anyone who works with him knows he is not moored to any discernible first principles that guide his decision making."
- "Meetings with him veer off topic and off the rails, he engages in repetitive rants, and his impulsiveness results in half-baked, ill-informed and occasionally reckless decisions that have to be walked back."
- "Given the instability many witnessed, there were early whispers within the cabinet of invoking the 25th Amendment, which would start a complex process for removing the president. But no one wanted to precipitate a constitutional crisis. So we will do what we can to steer the administration in the right direction until — one way or another — it's over."[75]

One could picture in their mind General Jack Ripper, the renegade B-52 base commander in *Dr. Strangelove*, played by Sterling Hayden, rambling on to his adjutant, Royal Air Force Group Captain Lionel Mandrake (Peter Sellers), about the dangers posed by fluoridation of the water supply:

"You know when fluoridation first began? Nineteen hundred and forty-six. Nineteen forty-six, Mandrake. How

---

[75] Anonymous, "I am Part of the Resistance Inside the Trump Administration," *The New York Times*, September 5, 2018.

does that coincide with your postwar commie conspiracy, huh? It's incredibly obvious, isn't it? A foreign substance is introduced into our precious bodily fluids without the knowledge of the individual, and certainly without any choice. That's the way your hard-core commie works."

As if the Anonymous piece in *The New York Times* was not enough to convince the world that the President of the United States was a complete psychotic idiot, what Woodward recounted in his book was enough to grab the attention of anyone with an ounce of common sense about them.

The comments made about Trump by some of his senior officials, all divulged by Woodward, would, under normal circumstances, result in a family intervening with mental health officials to have a relative committed to a psych ward.

Trump's dealing with other world leaders presented the psychological profile of a maniacal despot, in a manner reminiscent of Roman Emperor Caligula, Adolf Hitler, Joseph Stalin, and Uganda's Idi Amin. While many of Trump's most ardent right-wing supporters blamed an April 2017 chemical attack in Syria on a false flag operation by U.S., Turkish, Saudi, and Israeli forces to place blame on Syrian President Bashar al-Assad, Trump responded in a classic neocon manner.

According to Woodward's book, Trump said of Assad and his government, "Let's fucking kill him! Let's go in. Let's kill the fucking lot of them." Trump instructed Defense Secretary James Mattis to carry out the illegal assassination. Mattis replied that he would get right on it. Mattis then told his aide, "We're not going to do any of that. We're going to be much more measured."[76]

Mattis also had to contend with Trump's insistence on having a French Bastille Day-like military parade in Washington. Having witnessed the Bastille Day parade in Paris on July 14, 2017, Trump was jealous of President Macron. So, as with any petulant child, Trump wanted his own parade. The last such parade was one held by President George H. W. Bush after Operation Desert Storm in 1991.

The 1991 parade was held along Constitution Avenue and consisted of two M1-A1 Abrams tanks, each weighing 67-metric tons, and two 33-ton Bradley Fighting Vehicles. The parade resulted in disruption to DC's infrastructure, with street lights having to be removed and then re-installed and the armored vehicle treads from the tanks and Bradleys tearing up the asphalt along Constitution Avenue and side streets. Connecticut and Pennsylvania Avenues, as with many of DC's streets, were designed for a maximum of 30 gross weight tonnage per vehicle. None of these problems bothered Trump, who wanted to have his goddamned parade at any cost.

Another casualty of the 1991 parade was the Smithsonian's Hirshhorn Sculpture Garden. The only thing the attack helicopters over the Mall managed to "attack," with their rotor wash, were sculptures in the outdoor garden. Pebbles kicked up by the helicopters strafed the

---

[76] Woodward, *op. cit.*

sculptures, many of them priceless, with deep gouges. The total cost of parade damage for Washington was $12 million, not counting the destruction caused to the Hirshhorn.

When Egypt's Abdel Fattah el-Sisi brought up the investigation by Special Counsel Mueller in a phone call with Trump, Trump was insulted, later telling his personal attorney, John Dowd, that el-Sisi's comments, were a "kick in the nuts."[77]

Trump was livid over the one-two punch of the *New York Times* column and Woodward's book. He wanted the Justice Department to discover the identity of the anonymous writer based on frivolous national security grounds. And, Trump being his usual litigious self, dropped a warning in a September 5, 2018 tweet that he was considering suing Woodward and his publisher, Simon & Schuster, over the release of *Fear*. Trump tweeted, "Don't know why Washington politicians don't change libel laws?"

There is that pesky thing called the First Amendment that prevents a blowhard president like Trump from censoring journalists, book authors, or any other American.

Trump, who has the personality of an eight-year old spoiled brat, earned nothing but revulsion from White House staff, according to Woodward, Omarosa, Wolff, and many others. Woodward quotes Trump chief of staff John

---

[77] Woodward, *Ibid*.

Kelly as saying of Trump, "He's an idiot. It's pointless to try to convince him of anything. He's gone off the rails. We're in Crazytown. I don't even know why any of us are here. This is the worst job I've ever had."

The Insulter-in-Chief

Americans who voted for Trump may have believed they were getting a product of New York wealth – someone like a Franklin Roosevelt or a Nelson Rockefeller – who would kick the butts of Wall Street to get a better deal for the American middle class. What people got was a Don Rickles-like insulter who was incapable of empathy or modesty. In Rickles's case, his insult comedy routine was pure schtick – an act. Rickles, who died in 2017, was, in truth, a warm person off-stage. Trump, however, was never off-stage. His schtick was constant. Trump insulted people morning, noon, and night, whether from a podium or on Twitter.

If Trump was a run-of-the-mill bar patron, he would not get away with such insults for two minutes before someone got up and punched him in his pie hole. How many people wanted to reach into their TV screens during one of Trump's tirades and smack the living shit out of him? Trump could not count that high. While visiting the United Kingdom in July 2018, Trump pulled the rug out from under British Prime Minister Theresa May and divulged, in an interview with Rupert Murdoch's *Sun* newspaper, indicated that Britain's BREXIT withdrawal from the European Union was bolloxed up because May refused to listen to Trump's advice. Trump, breaking diplomatic protocol by airing a state-to-state conversation in public, said, "I would have done [BREXIT] much differently. I actually told Theresa May how to do it but she didn't agree, she didn't listen to me." Trump also endorsed May's then-Foreign Secretary, Boris Johnson, a Trump-like boor and former mayor of London, to succeed her as prime minister. It was a diplomatic affront that irritated most Britons, except for the xenophobes and racists of the British far-right, Trump's natural base on both sides of the Atlantic.

In June 2018, during tense trade negotiations at the White House, Trump insulted Japanese Prime Minister Shinzo Abe. Trump told Abe, "I remember Pearl Harbor," a reference to the December 7, 1941 Japanese attack on Hawaii, which launched the United States into World War II.[78] In any case, Trump was born in 1946, five years after the Pearl Harbor attack. However, in just five seconds, Trump managed to undo the trust built up between the United States and Japan ever since General Douglas MacArthur refused to exact crippling punishment on Japan, following its surrender in 1945.

Trump also had a nasty habit of calling Abe in what was mid-afternoon on the U.S. east coast, but in the middle of the night in Tokyo. With no idea of time zones, Trump would awaken Abe from his sleep. In 2017, during a briefing in preparation for a meeting with Indian Prime Minister Narendra Modi, Trump was shown a map of South Asia. Like some idiotic pre-adolescent boy, Trump

---

[78] John Hudson and Josh Dawsey, "'I remember Pearl Harbor': Inside Trump's hot-and-cold relationship with Japan's prime minister," *The Washington Post*, August 28, 2018.

insisted on pronouncing Nepal as "nipple" and Bhutan as "button."[79]

Trump's chairman of the National Economic Council, Gary Cohn, stole a document off Trump's desk before he had a chance to sign it. The document would have withdrawn the United States from a trade agreement with South Korea.[80]

Trump and his economic adviser, Larry Kudlow, nicknamed "crackhead Kudlow" for his cocaine addiction while a member of the Reagan administration, insulted Canadian Prime Minister Justin Trudeau. After the June 2018 G7 Summit in Canada, at which, Trump refused to sign the final communiqué, he tweeted that Trudeau was "dishonest & weak."

After Trump's tweet, his National Trade Council director, Peter Navarro, told Fox News Sunday that there was a "special place in hell" for any leader who engaged in bad faith diplomacy with Trump. On June 11, 2018, the Canadian House of Commons took the unprecedented step of officially condemning Trump, Navarro, and other administration advisers for their "disparaging ad hominem statements" about Trudeau. A unanimous vote against Trump's comments meant that every party represented in the House of Commons voted in favor of the diplomatic slap on the wrist of the Americans: Liberals, Conservatives,

---

[79] Daniel Lippman, "Trump's diplomatic learning curve: Time zones, 'Nambia' and 'Nipple,'" Politico, August 13, 2018.

[80] Woodward, *op. cit.*

New Democrats, Quebec Bloc, Greens, People's Party, and Independents. Donald Trump was quite a unifying factor. He galvanized countries, peoples, and parties against him and his administration.

While attending the plenary meeting of the UN General Assembly in New York in late September 2018, Trump pointedly refused to meet with Trudeau. In a typical rant, Trump said, he rejected a bilateral meeting with Trudeau, "because his tariffs are too high and he doesn't seem to want to move and I told him 'forget about it.'"[81]

At the same UN gathering in New York, Trump unloaded on French President Emmanuel Macron. Again, trade was the bee in Trump's bonnet. Trump's bilateral meeting with Macron was punctuated by Trump's "ranting and venting" on trade.[82]

Trump also had a rude comment about New Zealand's new prime minister, Jacinda Ardern, at the Asia Pacific Economic Cooperation (APEC) summit in Vietnam in November 2017. Not only did Trump reportedly mistake Ardern for Justin Trudeau's wife, but when he realized she was the new Labor Party prime minister of her country, he

---

[81] David Lawder, "Trump slams Canada over NAFTA, says rejected Trudeau meeting," Reuters, September 26, 2018.

[82] Michelle Kosinski and Jennifer Hansler, "Trump 'went off' on French President Emmanuel Macron in New York meeting," CNN, September 26, 2018.

patted her on the shoulder at the APEC dinner and said, "this lady caused a lot of upset in her country."

To Trump, any female leader caused him a lot of upset. Whether it was Germany's Angela Merkel (who Trump tweeted was "ruining Germany"), Britain's Theresa May and Queen Elizabeth, or New Zealand's Ardern, Trump had to demonstrate, like some aging stallion of a harem, his continued dominance.

Appearing on CNN after the G7, Crackhead Kudlow accused Trudeau of "stabbing" the United States in the back. A few months later, Kudlow hosted Peter Brimelow, the operator of the white supremacist website Vdare.com, at his annual birthday party bash. Vdare.com hosts articles by alt-rightists and anti-Semites.[83] Kudlow was born Jewish but converted to Catholicism in the 1990s.

The love affair between Jewish members of Trump's administration – Kudlow, Stephen Miller, and Jared Kushner – and alt-right anti-Semites was an enigma wrapped in a paradox and shrouded in a conundrum.

Many of Trump's acerbic insults, delivered in speeches and on Twitter, were to the FBI and Department and Justice. The history of U.S. crime bosses show that none held the

---

[83] Tucker Higgins and Eamon Javers, "Larry Kudlow hosted white nationalist publisher at birthday party, says he did not know his views," CNBC, August 21, 2018.

FBI or DOJ in high esteem, and crime boss Trump was no different.

Just after becoming president, Trump engaged in a shouting match in a phone call with Australian Prime Minister Malcolm Turnbull, which Trump abruptly ended after Trump called a refugee re-settlement agreement worked out between Barack Obama and Turnbull "dumb."

Trump's insulting bombast did hit one nail on the head, proving that a broken clock is correct twice a day. After sacking his White House "chief strategist" Steve Bannon, Trump called him "Sloppy Steve." In fact, Bannon did look like a homeless drunk on the street, often appearing at White House events disheveled, unshaven, and wearing clothing that looked like old remnants from Robert Hall. Trump's short-lived White House Director of Communications, Anthony Scaramucci, told an April 26, 2018 briefing at the National Press Club in Washington that Bannon looked like a "hobo."

Bannon began crisscrossing Europe after his departure from the White House. He was trying to drum up support for a Fourth Reich International, a Brussels-based neo-Nazi organization called "The Movement." The only movement Bannon -- a sort of overweight tramp version of Herman Goering, the obese Nazi Reich *Reichsmarschall* -- required was a bowel movement, since he was entirely full of shit.

Trump cared not for individuals who dedicated their entire lives to public service. He called former Vice President Joe Biden "Crazy Joe Biden," adding that Biden was "weak, both mentally and physically." A hallmark of a fascist demagogue, whether it was Hitler or his Nazi puppet henchmen throughout Europe, was to demean those with physical or mental disabilities or accuse their enemies of suffering from such conditions.

To Trump, Senator Dick Durbin, the Senate Minority Whip, was "Dicky Durbin." Senator Elizabeth Warren of Massachusetts was "Pocahontas" and "goofy Elizabeth Warren." The ranking member of the Senate Judiciary Committee, Dianne Feinstein, was "Sneaky Dianne." Former Secretary of State and 2016 Democratic presidential candidate Hillary Clinton was "Crooked Hillary." Senate Minority Leader Chuck Schumer became "Cryin' Chuck" to Trump. Arizona Republican Senator Jeff Flake was Jeff Flake(y). Representative Maxine Waters (D-CA) was "Crazy Maxine." Representative Frederica Wilson (D-FL) became "Wacky Congresswoman Wilson." After incoming House Intelligence Committee Democratic chairman Adam Schiff (D-CA) berated Trump for appointing Matt Whitaker as assistant Attorney General without Senate confirmation, Trump formulated a 6th grade-level for Schiff in a tweet: "So funny to see little Adam Schitt (D-CA) talking about the fact that Acting Attorney General Matt Whitaker was not approved by the Senate . . . but not mentioning the fact that Bob Mueller (who is highly conflicted) was not approved by the Senate!"

A little over a half-hour later, Schiff responded to Trump on Twitter: "Wow, Mr. President, that's a good one. Was that like your answers to Mr. Mueller's questions, or did you write this one yourself?"

Representative Conor Lamb (D-PA), who defeated a Republican in a 2018 special election in a district Trump won by almost 20 points, became "Lamb the Sham" in Trump's insult lexicon. Martin O'Malley, the former governor of Maryland, was called a "clown" and the "failed former Mayor of Baltimore" in a Trump tweet. Vermont Senator Bernie Sanders was "Crazy Bernie" to Trump.

Even members of Trump's own administration were not spared the incessant insults. Attorney General Jeff Sessions became "Mr. Magoo" and Deputy Attorney General Rod Rosenstein was "Mr. Peepers." According to Woodward's book, Trump said of Sessions, "This guy is mentally retarded. He's this dumb Southerner . . . He couldn't even be a one-person country lawyer down in Alabama."[84]

That fascist tendency by Trump was on full display at a campaign event in South Carolina in November 2015. Referring to *New York Times* reporter Serge Kovaleski, born with deformities in his hands and arms, Trump mocked his disability by saying, "you've got to see this guy," and curling his arms and hands in an attempt to impersonate Kovaleski, added, "Ah, I don't know what I said! I don't remember!"[85] The incident represented one of the lowest points, up to that time, in American politics.

Trump called ABC News commentator Cokie Roberts "kooky Cokie Roberts." It is more than likely that Trump

---

[84] Woodward, *op. cit.*
[85] Tony Dokoupil and Joy Y. Wang, "Trump appears to mock a person with disabilities. Again." MSNBC, November 27, 2015.

never heard of Roberts's father, the late House Majority Leader Hale Boggs, who disappeared on a plane flying over Alaska in 1973, or her mother, Lindy Boggs, who succeeded her husband in the House of Representatives in 1973.

Some of America's finest actors also came in for disgusting insults from Trump, usually in the form of tweets. Trump tweeted the following about Robert DeNiro: "Robert De Niro, a very Low IQ individual, has received too many shots to the head by real boxers in movies. I watched him last night and truly believe he may be 'punch-drunk.' I guess he doesn't realize the economy is the best it's ever been with employment being at an all time high, and many companies pouring back into our country. Wake up Punchy!"

DeNiro played boxer Jake LaMotta in the 1980 black-and-white bio-pic *Raging Bull*. The author met DeNiro in Washington, DC on December 2, 2014 and briefly discussed our past encounters with LaMotta. Having spoken with DeNiro and having had covered some of Trump speeches during the 2016 campaign, an honest observation is that the person who sounded "punch drunk" was Trump. He was rambling, boisterous, and repetitive.

And, since Trump was familiar with *Raging Bull*, hence his reference to DeNiro being "punch drunk," perhaps a nice retort to the insulting bastard who sat in the White House should have been DeNiro's line from the movie: "I'm gonna open his hole like this. Please excuse my French. I'm gonna make him suffer. I'm gonna make his mother wish she never had him - make him into dog meat."

"The hair is real - it's the head that's a fake"- Steve Allen

Television performers were not spared by the Insulter-in-Chief. Trump tweeted about them: "Late Night host are dealing with the Democrats for their very 'unfunny' & repetitive material, always anti-Trump! Should we get Equal Time?" Trump was obviously not aware that even during the time of the Federal Communications Commission's "Fairness Doctrine," which provided equal time for those with opposing political view to appear on television and radio stations, the rule never applied to late night television hosts like Johnny Carson, Jack Paar, Dick Cavett, Merv Griffin, Steve Allen, or David Frost. The great Steve Allen is memorable for two quotes that certainly apply to Trump: "The hair is real - it's the head that's a fake" and "Totalitarianism is patriotism institutionalized."

Whether it was politics, international relations, entertainment, or professional sports, Trump could always find something insulting to day about someone. During the flap over football players kneeling during the playing of the pre-game national anthem, Trump, who was once barred by the National Football League from buying the Buffalo Bills, tweeted the following about National Football League Commissioner Roger Goodell: "Can you believe that the disrespect for our Country, our Flag, our Anthem continues without penalty to the players. The Commissioner has lost control of the hemorrhaging league. Players are the boss!"

Trump also tweeted this about Major League Baseball, an American institution: "Can't believe Major League Baseball just rejected @PeteRose_14 for the Hall of Fame. He's paid the price. So ridiculous - let him in!" To Trump, it did not matter whether one broke the rules of baseball, or the stock market, or political campaigns, or the law in general. They were just fine in his book.

Trump's criticisms of department stories like Macy's and Nordstrom put a target on the back of every shopper who could have been confronted by some wild-eyed kook armed with a gun who wanted to "have the president's back."

Labor union officials were always a target for Trump, who regularly failed to pay his construction workers and had nothing but disdain for organized, except for mob-run unions that built his condos and casinos in New York, Atlantic City, and Las Vegas. This is what Trump tweeted about Steelworkers Union local president Chuck Jones, who realized that Trump's promise to have Carrier, the air conditioning manufacturer, keep its plant in Indiana and not move it to Mexico was pure bunkum: "Chuck Jones, who is President of United Steelworkers 1999, has done a terrible job representing workers. No wonder companies flee country!"

One thing that fascist dictators have in common is that they always attempt to place their personal imprimatur on all social and cultural events and customs that make up their nation's core. Trump believed that constitutionally-protected protests in America were aimed at him and should, therefore, be illegal and punishable.

Hurricane Trump

After Hurricane Maria devastated Puerto Rico in September 2017, Donald Trump paid a five-hour visit to the storm-ravaged and devastated commonwealth territory of the United States. The presidential trip came a full two weeks after the storm left 93 percent of the 3.5 million people of the island without power a sizable portion without clean drinking water. How did Trump respond to this disaster?

First, he complained about how the disaster relief for the commonwealth was busting the federal budget, as if Puerto Ricans were not worthy of the assistance afforded to the people of Texas. Louisiana, and Florida after two other hurricanes. Trump, lacking an ounce of empathy, told Puerto Rico, "you've thrown our budget a little out of whack... but that's fine."

Then came the biggest insult. Trump, visiting a disaster relief center at Calvary Chapel in San Juan, decided to toss rolls of paper towels to Puerto Ricans in the audience of what was a gaudy public relations stunt.

Trump then engaged in an unforgivable attempt to politicize the death count from the storm in Puerto Rico. Trump said, "Every death is a horror, but if you look at a real catastrophe like Katrina, and you look at the tremendous -- hundreds and hundreds and hundreds of people that died." Trump then asked Governor Ricardo

Rossello, "What is your death count as of this moment . . . seventeen?"

Almost boasting as if he had achieved a great golf score, Trump was told the number was sixteen. Trump replied, "Sixteen people certified . . . sixteen people versus in the thousands. You can be very proud of all of your people and all of our people working together. Sixteen versus literally thousands of people. You can be very proud." The official death count had doubled to 34 as Trump was cheering his success at keeping the total to 16.

For San Juan's Popular Democratic Party mayor Carmen Yulin Cruz, Trump's comments and actions were outrageous. She was not alone. Anyone with any compassion understood that Trump was making a public relations and campaign spectacle out of the death and despair in Puerto Rico and the neighboring U.S. Virgin Islands. Mayor Cruz, who was traveling throughout San Juan rendering municipal assistance to those who had lost everything came in for personal attacks from the hyper-misogynist Trump. Even before traveling to Puerto Rico, Trump tweeted about Cruz, writing, that she "really did not do a very good job in fact did a very poor job." Trump also tweeted, "Such poor leadership ability by the Mayor of San Juan, and others in Puerto Rico, who are not able to get their workers to help."

Trump's cronies also attempted to turn a profit from the misery endured by Puerto Rico.

Whitefish, Montana, population 6,500, was the home of Interior Secretary Ryan Zinke, an ex-Navy SEAL, who retired under an ethical cloud, and the former home of white supremacist and neo-Nazi Richard Spencer, a college pal of Trump's speechwriter, Stephen Miller. Whitefish was also the home of Whitefish Energy, a three-person firm that landed and then lost a $300 million contract to restore Puerto Rico's energy grid after Hurricane Maria. Whitefish Energy was owned by Andy Techmanski, a friend of Zinke. Techmanski hired Zinke's son during the summer of 2017 at one of his construction sites in Montana. Lola Zinke, Secretary Zinke's wife, was the main intermediary between Techmanski and the Interior Secretary in steering the Puerto Rico power grid contract to Whitefish Energy. That contract was later canceled after protests in Puerto Rico and on the mainland.

On October 1, 2017, as Puerto Rico continued counting its dead from Maria, Trump tweeted: "We have done a great job with the almost impossible situation in Puerto Rico. Outside of the Fake News or politically motivated ingrates . . ."

For a rank racist like Trump, Puerto Ricans, Mexicans, Central Americans, and anyone who wasn't a billionaire Latin American oligarch were just lazy.

But you could also be a resident of Texas and be insulted by Trump in the aftermath of a disastrous hurricane. Almost a year after Hurricane Harvey, which devastated Texas with unprecedented flooding, Trump said, in a conference call with federal and state officials preparing for the 2018 hurricane season, said, "Sixteen thousand people, many of them in Texas, for whatever reason that is. People went out in their boats to watch the hurricane. That didn't work out too well."

Once again, Trump lied about a disaster. No one had gone out in boats to watch the hurricane. The only people who "went out in their boats" were the U.S. Coast Guard, the volunteer "Cajun Navy" from Louisiana, and civilian organizations, which, together, rescued 46,000 people and thousands of pets. [86]

Almost a year after Maria, Harvey, and Irma, as another powerful hurricane, Florence, bore down on the Carolina coast, Trump decided to engage in more hurricane death count one-upmanship antics. One the morning of September 12, 2018, Trump tweeted: "We got A Pluses for our recent hurricane work in Texas and Florida (and did an unappreciated great job in Puerto Rico, even though an inaccessible island with very poor electricity and a totally

---

[86] Andrea Zelinski and St. John Barned-Smith, "Trump: Many Texans watched Harvey from their boats, requiring Coast Guard rescue," *Houston Chronicle*, June 7, 2018.

incompetent Mayor of San Juan). We are ready for the big one that is coming."

The Puerto Rican government had commissioned a scientific study of the actual death count from Maria in Puerto Rico. The conclusion by the Milken Institute School of Public Health at George Washington University was that the hurricane-related death county stood at 2,975. Other experts at Harvard University put the total death toll at 4,645, more than those killed in the 9/11 attacks and Katrina combined.

Trump decided that the actual death count number issued by the Puerto Rican government, 2,975, was inflated by Democrats to hurt his image. It did not matter that Governor Rossello was a member of the pro-statehood party linked to the GOP.[87] On September 13, 2018, Trump tweeted: "3000 people did not die in the two hurricanes that hit Puerto Rico. When I left the Island, AFTER the storm had hit, they had anywhere from 6 to 18 deaths. As time went by it did not go up by much. Then, a long time later, they started to report really large numbers, like 3000 . . . This was done by the Democrats in order to make me look as bad as possible when I was successfully raising

---

[87] In a September 24, 2018 interview with Geraldo Rivera on WTAM radio in Cleveland, Trump said about statehood, "With the mayor of San Juan [Carmen Yulin Cruz] as bad as she is and as incompetent as she is, Puerto Rico shouldn't be talking about statehood until they get some people that really know what they're doing," adding, "With people like that involved in Puerto Rico, I would be an absolute no." In other words, if any state or territory failed to produce leaders that walked in lock-step with Trump, their statehood status could be questioned.

Billions of Dollars to help rebuild Puerto Rico. If a person died for any reason, like old age, just add them onto the list. Bad politics."

Mayor Cruz had a terse Twitter response about Trump's comments: "Simply put: delusional, paranoid, and unhinged from any sense of reality. Trump is so vain he thinks this is about him. NO IT IS NOT." Just as Trump constantly called the press "fake news," he decided to traipse down the conspiracy path of "fake death counts." Of course, for an imbecile like Trump and his equally-imbecilic "base," everything was fake or a hoax: the news, man-made climate change, and a federal criminal probe of Trump's election campaign racketeering.

Trump said he believed that man-made climate change was a "Chinese hoax." In truth, Trump was one giant hoax on the entire planet. Someone with such a lack of basic curiosity about science should never again be permitted to tarnish the Oval Office.

The New York Daily News editorial board summed up the disgust many Americans shared about Trump's intemperate remarks about the Puerto Rico death count, as over a million people were evacuating the coast of the Carolinas ahead of Florence, "The President of the United States is a disgusting individual with a dysfunctional moral compass . . . We have a President with chronic distemper who runs roughshod over the rule of law and democratic norms, but asks to be judged by results. When the results do not fit the narrative he wishes to advance, he attacks facts as political fabrication."[88]

Hurricanes Maria & Trump

Trump was not over arguing about the death count in Puerto Rico from Maria.

As Florence was battering the Carolinas, Trump tweeted, on September 14, 2018, questioning *The Washington Post's* reporting on the storm's total death count, "When Trump visited the island territory last October, OFFICIALS told him in a briefing 16 PEOPLE had died from Maria." The Washington Post. This was long AFTER the hurricane took place. Over many months it went to 64 PEOPLE. Then, like magic, "3000 PEOPLE KILLED." They hired . . . GWU[89] Research to tell them how many people had died in Puerto Rico (how would they not know this?). This method was never done with previous hurricanes because other jurisdictions know how many people were killed. FIFTY TIMES LAST ORIGINAL NUMBER - NO WAY!"

For Trump, a peer-reviewed study commissioned by the government of Puerto Rico that concluded 2,975 people

---

[88] New York Daily News Editorial Board, "Hurricane Donald: The President is a bad man," *The New York Daily News*, September 13, 2018.

[89] George Washington University in Washington, DC.

died from hurricane-related causes on the island was some sort of "conspiracy theory." In May 2018, a Harvard University study commissioned by the prestigious New England Journal of Medicine concluded that an estimated average of 4,465 people in Puerto Rico likely died from Maria-related causes.[90] Trump's delusions about the deaths of American citizens were roundly condemned, even by the usually supine members of his own party. Trump's ignorance of facts became an actual national security threat to the United States.

And how did Trump deal with the costs of cleaning up from Hurricanes Irma and Harvey? He called on Congress to pass tax cuts for billionaires, even as his administration was failing to provide financial assistance to those who lost their homes and small businesses. Trump tweeted the following on September 13, 2017: "With Irma and Harvey devastation, Tax Cuts and Tax Reform is needed more than ever before. Go Congress, go!"

---

[90] Emma Schwartz, Hurricane Maria's New Death Toll Estimate Is Higher Than Katrina's," Frontline, August 28, 2018.

[90] Daniel Lippman and Eliana Johnson, "Trump's FEMA chief under investigation over use of official cars," Politico, September 13, 2018.

And what would the Trump administration's coordinator of disaster relief be without an abuser of the public trust? As the Carolinas were under several feet of water from Hurricane Florence, it was disclosed that Brock Long, Trump's director of the Federal Emergency Management Agency (FEMA), misused government resources, including government vehicles and personnel, on private weekend trips from Washington, DC to his home in Hickory, North Carolina.[91] One didn't have to be Barney Fife, the deputy sheriff of television's fictional North Carolina town of Mayberry (played by Don Knotts),[92] to tell Homeland Security Secretary Kirstjen Nielsen that when it came to Long, it was time to just "nip it in the bud!"

Long, a GOP political crony from Alabama, was more interested in fleecing the taxpayers than in doing his job. For example, over a year after Maria, the island of Vieques, off the east coast of Puerto Rico, was still operating on generators. The island had received a mere

---

[92] Knotts's co-star, Andy Griffith, who played Mayberry's Sheriff Andy Taylor on *The Andy Griffith Show*, earned hate messages from the right-wing when, in 2010, he cut a commercial ad extolling the Affordable Care Act. Even Mayberry was not American enough for the despicable cretins of the metastasizing Republican Party.

$260,000 from FEMA for hurricane relief and recovery.[93] In comparison, Trump's travel costs to his Mar-a-Lago resort in Florida and his golf clubs in New Jersey and Virginia cost the taxpayers over $13 million for 2017 alone.

When Barney Fife had the answer to all the ills in the Trump administration – nip them all in the bud – did the total failure of the American political and legal systems become more than apparent.

On a visit to hard-hit North Carolina in the wake of Florence, Trump was more concerned about the flood stage of Lake Norman than over the fact that many thousands of people had lost their homes in flood waters. Trump asked a North Carolina official, "How is Lake Norman doing?" The reason was that a Trump National Golf Club was near the lake. Handing out box lunches to storm evacuees, Trump told one man, as he handed him his box lunch, "Have a good time." Trump told another man, who witnessed a yacht that had careened into his house, "At least you got a nice boat out of the deal."[94]

To the White House staff, Trump became an emperor without clothes. *Politico* reported that West Wing officials

---

[93] CBS News, "Forgotten island: Vieques still running entirely on generators more than a year after Maria hit," September 22, 2018.

[94] Margaret Hartmann, "Trump to Hurricane Florence Survivor: 'Have a Good Time,'" *Daily Intelligencer*, September 20, 2018.

decided that it was fruitless to convince Trump top stop tweeting and revealed, "After 20 months of failed efforts to corral the president, it's best to let the president – who has long viewed himself as his best spokesman, strategist and negotiator – say what he wants to say and move on."[95]

In October 2017, after a gunman opened fire into a crowd of concert attendees from a hotel window on the Las Vegas Strip, killing 59 and wounding hundreds of others, Trump tweeted: "My warmest condolences and sympathies to the victims and families of the terrible Las Vegas shooting. God bless you!" What the hell did Trump think he was sending? A fucking greeting card?

In October 2018, after a far-right gunman massacred eleven worshippers at the Tree of Life synagogue in the Squirrel Hill neighbor of Pittsburgh, Pennsylvania, a visiting Trump and Melania offered no words of condolence to the congregation but spoke of how well he and the First Lady were treated upon their arrival in Pittsburgh. Not present to welcome Trump were the Governor of Pennsylvania or the Mayor of Pittsburgh. Trump was not wanted in Pittsburgh following the mass shooting, but he forced himself upon the city and later claimed that his reception could not have been better.

---

[95] Andrew Restuccia, Christopher Cadelago, and Matthew Choi, "West Wing aides perfect a Trump survival skill: Ignoring the tweets," *Politico*, September 13, 2018.

In the devastated California town of Paradise, wiped out from raging forest fires, Trump, on a "morale-boosting" visit, referred twice to the town as "Pleasure." Clearly, Mr. Trump's twisted and perverted mind was across the state line in Nevada in some brothel.

When it came to one of the major presidential roles – "consoler-in-chief" – Trump earned a big fat "F."

Trump's Twilight Zone

Just when normal Americans believed no one could be more of an idiot than Donald Trump, out popped some self-appointed "expert" on various lunatic conspiracy theories from Trump's "base." They appeared at Trump rallies, on Fox News, on right-wing talk radio, and on fringe websites. These people could have walked from the set of any episode of Rod Serling's *Twilight Zone*.

While, on the subject of movies and science fiction, how many Americans knew that the villainous Biff Tannen character, played by Thomas Wilson) in the *Back to the Future* trilogy, was based by screenwriter Bob Gale on none other than Donald Trump?

In *Back to the Future Part II*, Tannen, who was the antagonist of Marty McFly (Michael J. Fox) is shown as a successful casino tycoon, who has bought influence throughout the government and is involved as a crime boss lording over a city of graft and crime. Just as Donald Trump used Trump Foundation money to have a massive portrait of himself painted, Tannen's office is graced by a similar portrait. Biff amasses his great wealth because McFly, in *Back to the Future I*, mistakenly leaves a sports almanac from 1985 in the year 1955. After Biff finds it, he proceeds to bet on as many sports matches as possible, which makes him a gazillionaire.

Trump didn't have to find a sports almanac from the future to make his millions in casinos and hotels. He had the mob and his wealthy father, Fred Trump, Sr., looking out for interests, in addition to mob lawyer and notorious right-wing Republican asshole Roy Cohn to grease the skids for his business success.

Trump was, rolled up into one villainous bastard, Henry F. Potter, the miserly old banker, played by Lionel Barrymore in Frank Capra's Christmas classic, *It's a Wonderful Life*; Biff Tannen in *BTTF II*; and Auric Goldfinger, played by Gert Fröbe, in the James Bond movie, *Goldfinger*. Unlike Goldfinger, the man with the "Midas touch," Trump's touch was in reverse. Everything that Trump touched turned into a pile of shit.

And if Bob Gale didn't have a window on future events, what about Ingersoll Lockwood. In the 1890s, Lockwood, a novelist, who also happened to be a lawyer and political columnist, wrote two illustrated children's books titled, respectively, *The Travels and Adventures of Little Baron Trump and His Wonderful Dog Bulgar* and *Baron Trump's Marvelous Underground Journey*. The main character is a fabulously wealthy young lad named "Baron Trump," who lives in Castle Trump. Baron embarks on various voyages, including a trip to Russia to discover a gateway to an alternate dimension. All the time, Baron Trump is guided by the "master of all masters," a person named "Don."

In 1896, Lockwood completed his trilogy with something that should make us all sit up and pay attention. His final book, titled *1900, Or The Last President*, published by the American News Company, is set in a New York City engulfed in violence from workers who have been pushed to the edge by the city's elite class. A police curfew has

been imposed on the city and the United States verges on the brink of collapse. The first location that is set upon by an angry mob is the Fifth Avenue Hotel, which sits between 56th and 57th Streets. Ready for this? It is the very same address where the Trump Tower stands today. Of course, Trump's son is named Barron, but the similarities between today and the turn-of-the-19th century era work of fiction are uncanny.[96]

The White House veered into an utterly looney conversation about "alternate universes," during a bizarre October 11, 2018 Oval Office meeting between Trump, Jared Kushner, Ivanka Trump, and rap artist Kanye West. West, to a stunned Oval Office entourage, said, "So there's a theory that -- there's infinite amounts of universe and there's alternate universe so it's very important for me to get [Larry] Hoover out, because in an alternate universe, I

---

[96] Chris Riotta, "Did an Author from the 1800s Predict the Trumps, Russia and America's Downfall?" *Newsweek*, July 31, 2017.

am him and I have to go and get him free." Larry Hoover had been the leader of the Chicago street gang, the Gangster Disciples," before he was sentenced in 1997 to a maximum 200-year sentence at the federal Supermax prison in Florence, Colorado. West had appealed to Trump to grant Hoover clemency.

One thing that Trump did not mind destroying in our own reality was planet Earth. On June 1, 2017, Trump announced that the United States was withdrawing from the Paris climate change accord of April 22, 2016 (Earth Day). The United States became the sole pariah in rejecting the accord. Every other nation, including North Korea, China, Vatican City, and Iran, acceded to the accord.

At a September 2018 meeting in San Francisco of the Global Climate Action Summit, California Governor Jerry Brown castigated Trump's environmental policies, saying that Trump was a "liar, criminal, fool, pick your choice." Like the evil Ming the Merciless, played by Charles B. Middleton, in the *Flash Gordon* film serials of the 1930s, Trump seemed intent on wreaking havoc on the Earth by embracing the dirtiest and foulest of energy sources.

These included Trump's fanatical embrace of coal-fired power plants, drilling in environmentally-sensitive areas, and allowing uranium miners access to Bears Ears and Grand Staircase-Escalante National Monuments – sacred to Native Americans.

Like the Borg Collective in the *Star Trek* television series, Trump was the Borg Queen, intent on sucking up every natural resource from the planet, leaving behind pollution and environmental devastation on behalf of Trump's "collective" of crooks, gangsters, and fraudsters. Perhaps that is why Trump ordered the creation of a U.S. Space Force, something that was not wanted by the Pentagon or the Air Force.

The Space Force was also a violation of the 1967 Treaty on Principles Governing the Activities of States in the Exploration and Use of Outer Space, including the Moon and Other Celestial Bodies, known simply as the "Outer Space Treaty." The treaty established the basis for international space law. Basic laws of behavior were not Trump's cup of tea, as seen in his willingness to make unconstitutional end runs around the U.S. Congress, the federal judiciary, and the states.

Since 1967, 107 nations joined the United States, the United Kingdom, and the Soviet Union (succeeded in ratification by Russia in fully ratified the treaty, which bans the placement of weapons of mass destruction in Earth orbit and the establishment of military bases, installations, and fortifications on the Moon and other celestial bodies.

Trump's creation of a military Space Force also supplanted the civilian-operated National Aeronautics and Space Administration (NASA) overseeing U.S. space operations.

Trump's call for space to be a "new warfighting domain" effectively violated pre-existing U.S. treaty obligations.

Trump transformed the United States into a version of the fictional banana republic of San Marcos, the locale in Woody Allen's 1971 comedy, *Bananas*. The annual custom in the country is that each citizen of San Marcos presents his Excellency, the dictator-president, with his weight in horse manure. In Trump's "bananas republic," the would-be dictator-president presents every American citizen his or her weight in horse manure, on a daily basis.

The main character in *Bananas*, Fielding Mellish (Allen) becomes involved in a coup d'état carried about by San Marcos revolutionaries against the caudillo. Mellish, an American who travels to San Marcos, and, resulting from a comedy of events, is selected as the president of the country. Mellish returns to the United States to ask for aid for "his country." The U.S. government brings charges against Mellish for being an imposter president of San Marcos.

The news of Mellish's arrest leads the evening broadcast:

Rudy (in drag) and The Beast – Great GOP "family values"

"Good evening. I'm Roger Grimsby with the news at six. Today's top stories:

The United States government brings charges against Fielding Mellish as a subversive impostor, New York garbage men are striking for a better class of garbage, and the National Rifle Association declares death a good thing." Life imitating art? The NRA, with Trump's support, seems to revel in every mass shooting because it can push for more gun sales. The more deaths the better for the NRA. Trump ordered his administration to step up anti-government activities in Venezuela, Nicaragua, and Cuba.

Mellish's defense at his trial sounded like Trump's deranged tweets regarding the probe of his campaign by special prosecutor Mueller: "I object, your honor! This trial is a travesty. It's a travesty of a mockery of a sham of a mockery of a travesty of two mockeries of a sham." Trump and his Sylvester the Cat-sounding and cross-dressing mouthpiece, Rudolph Giuliani, couldn't have said it better.

On August 19, 2018, Giuliani, acting as Trump's lawyer, appeared on NBC's *Meet the Press*. Host Chuck Todd, responding to Giuliani's insistence that Trump should not testify before special prosecutor Mueller, said, "Truth is truth." Giuliani replied, "No, no, it isn't truth . . . Truth isn't truth." The verbal interchange demonstrated, once again, that the United States had embarked down a fantasy road of lunacy mixed with a vile strategy of dealing in disinformation.

There is one other cogent message regarding Trump's Twilight Zone. During the fiasco of the Kavanaugh confirmation hearing, the following tweet was sent on September 28, 2018 by Anne Serling, the daughter of *The*

Twilight Zone's creator Rod Serling and author of *As I Knew Him: My Dad, Rod Serling*:

"Because *The Twilight Zone* has been invoked in the Kavanaugh hearings, I'll offer this: my father believed in decency, integrity and justice. Had he written this, I assure you--there would indeed be a further FBI investigation along with some cosmic justice."

Earlier, during the morning of September 28, a group of moderate Republicans and Democrats agreed to make a slight attempt at tripping up the nomination of Kavanaugh, who, a day earlier, had engaged in a bitter right-wing screed against the Democrats, Clinton, and a "left-wing conspiracy." The FBI was authorized to conduct a constrained investigation of Kavanaugh's background. Kavanaugh's performance before the Senate Judiciary Committee the prior day was right out of *The Twilight Zone*.

One episode of *The Twilight Zone* was particularly germane to the Trump administration. That episode, "He's Alive." Which aired in January 1963, featured a young Dennis Hopper as a street-brawling American neo-Nazi named Peter Vollmer. On a darkened city street, Vollmer is approached by a shadowy figure who urges him to fight on and claim that white people were the endangered minority. The figure was the ghost of Adolf Hitler. After convincing Vollmer to commit murder, the ghostly Fuehrer looks for another "volunteer" to spread his message of hate. Rod Serling then said something about the Hitler specter that was as cogent in 1963 as it was in 2018:

"Where will he go next, this phantom from another time, this resurrected ghost of a previous nightmare – Chicago? Los Angeles? Miami, Florida? Vincennes, Indiana? Syracuse, New York? Anyplace, everyplace, where there's hate, where there's prejudice, where there's bigotry. He's alive. He's alive so long as these evils exist. Remember that when he comes to your town. Remember it when you hear his voice speaking out through others. Remember it when you hear a name called, a minority attacked, any blind, unreasoning assault on a people or any human being. He's alive because through these things we keep him alive."

That specter was alive and well during every one of Trump's "campaign rallies" that were held across the country and were nothing more than hate fests, of which Hitler would have been proud to see occur in the world's largest cradle of democracy. One of Trump's favorite orchestrations was to fire up his crowd by denouncing certain political opponents, to which the crowd, which included many paid attendees, responded by shouting, "Lock her up!" The targets of this mob hollering included Hillary Clinton, Senator Dianne Feinstein (D-CA), and House Minority Leader Nancy Pelosi.

In a June 2018 tweet, in which he was venting his spleen about leakers, Trump wrote: "Leakers are traitors and cowards, and we will find out who they are!" Interestingly, Hitler once said of his enemies, "Cowards! Traitors and cowards!" It should be stated that Trump was never original in anything he said.

The entire Trump administration and what it wrought for the United States was the plot line from a novel or film about an eerie alternate reality. I can speak for myself and several colleagues who, since the election of Trump, have lost friendships, some lasting more than thirty years. It was not a normal Republican-Democratic divide that placed these friendships on the rocks, but the insistence by some formerly well-meaning people, caught up in a national hate frenzy, that Trump was what was best for the country. History records such echoes from the past: in Berlin, Danzig, Vienna, and Frankfurt in the 1920s and 30s.

The loss of friendships during the Joseph McCarthy-inspired witch hunts of the 1950s was featured as a subliminal political message in the 1956 sci-fi classic, *Invasion of the Body Snatchers*. Dr. Miles J. Bennell, played by actor Kevin McCarthy (not to be confused with the banal GOP House Majority Whip Kevin McCarthy),[97] said, "In my practice, I've seen how people have allowed their humanity to drain away. Only it happened slowly instead of all at once. They didn't seem to mind . . . All of us -- a little bit -- we harden our hearts, grow callous. Only when

---

[97] Unlike the buffoonish Republican congressman from California, the actor Kevin McCarthy served in the U.S. military, distinguishing himself in the U.S. Army Air Corps in World War II.

we have to fight to stay human do we realize how precious it is to us, how dear."

In the age of Trump, many of us fought successfully to stay human, while others, many of them our family and friends, succumbed to the worst instincts of humanity: fear of "the other," hatred, greed, and capitulation to a tyrant who relied only on gimmickry to maintain his baseline of support.

I was not the only American who dearly wanted to wake up from the nightmare brought about by Donald Trump. As America's institutions of governance and the rule of law – the FBI, the Justice Department, the U.S. Supreme Court, the U.S. Congress, the State Department, the military, the public commons, etc. – all fell victim to Trumpian policies, there was no waking from the nightmare but a steadfast desire by righteous and decent Americans to rid the nation, once and for all, of the hate politics manifested by the Trump administration. It was not America's first dalliance with such policies, but it had to damned well be the last.

And that concludes our frightful and a bit of a comedic dispatch (because without some laughter, this crazy situation would have been far too much to bear) from Trump's Twilight Zone, which can be found just down the road and around the corner from Trump's Bananas Republic.

🍌🍌🍌🍌🍌🍌🍌🍌🍌🍌🍌🍌

Index

Abe, Shinzo, 98, 179
Abrams, Stacey, 162, 175
Allen, Steve, 187
Allen, Woody, 207
Andres, Greg, 114
Ardern, Jacinda, 181, 182
Asia Pacific Economic Cooperation, 181
Assad, Bashar al, 49, 50, 54, 174
Baldwin, Alec, 81
Bannon, Steve, 20, 21, 23, 67, 98, 136, 183
Barrymore, Lionel, 203
Bates, Kathy, 160
Bernstein, Robin, 67
Bialystock, Max, 116, 117
Biden, Joe, 23, 24, 183
Bilko, Ernest G., 126
bin Salman, Mohammed, 132
Blackburn, Marsha, 13, 20
Bogart, Humphrey, 144
Bolsonaro, Jair, 138
Bolton, John, 47, 48, 51, 63
Bond, James, 135, 203
Bondevik, Kjell Magne, 74
Booker, Cory, 157
Bornstein, Dr. Harold, 152
Brennan, John, 159
Brinkema, Leonie, 156, 157
Brown, Jerry, 205
Brown, Scott, 69
Bunker, Archie, 154, 155

Bush, George W., 26, 50, 64, 118
Buttram, Pat, 44
Caan, James, 160
Caligula, Emperor, 32, 33, 174
Cambridge Analytica, 135, 137, 142
Capra, Frank, 203
Carlson, Tucker, 60
Carson, Ben, 117, 118, 133
Chao, Elaine, 127
Christie, Chris, 110
Clapper, James, 159
Claudius, Emperor, 32, 33, 34
Clinton, Hillary, 37, 81, 89, 140, 141, 149, 184
Cobblepot, Oswald, 112, 113
Comey, James, 113, 114, 147, 149, 159
Cruz, Carmen Yulin, 61, 191, 194
Daniels, Stormy, 82
DeNiro, Robert, 186, 187
DeSantis, Ron, 97, 98
DesJarlais, Scott, 13, 19
DeVos, Betsy, 35, 36, 37, 65, 70, 118
Dick, Philip K., 161
Dobson, James, 9, 10
Donohue, Sean, 96
Dowd, John, 176

Dreyfuss, Richard, 40
Duque, Ivan, 115, 116
Durbin, Dick, 184
Ecclestone, Diana, 68
el-Sisi, Abdel Fattah, 176
Epstein, Jeffrey, 100, 141
Falwell, Jerry, 133, 134
Federal Emergency Management Agency, 79, 198
Feinstein, Dianne, 184
Fife, Barney, 198, 199
Fitzgerald, John, 97
Flake, Jeff, 184
Fransen, Jayda, 155
Freedom Caucus, 13, 16, 19, 27
Fröbe, Gert, 203
Gaetz, Matt, 13, 15, 16, 17, 27
Gianforte, Greg, 93
Gillum, Andrew, 97, 162
Giuliani, Rudolph, 140, 208
Gohmert, Louis, 18, 19, 27
Goldfinger, 126, 203
Golding, Paul, 20
Goldwater, Barry, 37, 134
Goodell, Roger, 188
Gorka, Sebastian, 20, 21, 22, 23, 98
Gorsuch, Neil, 40, 41
Greenblatt, Jason, 49
Grenell, Richard, 63, 64, 67
Grossman, Seth, 96
Guthrie, Woody, 103
Haley, Nikki, 46, 117, 163
Hastert, Dennis, 17, 37
Hatch, Orrin, 42
Hayden, Michael, 159
Hayden, Sterling, 173
Heston, Charlton, 25, 128
Hitler, Adolf, 20, 28, 30, 77, 96, 97, 123, 171, 174, 184, 209, 210
Howell III, Thurston, 129
Hurricane Maria, 190, 192, 193, 194, 196, 197, 198, 199
Huston, Walter, 40
Hutchison, Kay Bailey, 125, 126
International Criminal Court, 54, 128
James, LeBron, 161
Jeffress, Robert, 134
Johnson, Boris, 179
Jones, Arthur, 96
Jordan, Jim, 16, 27, 37
Kasowitz, Benson, Torres & Friedman, 47, 49
Kavanaugh, Brett, 40, 41, 42, 43, 44, 86, 208, 209
Kennedy, John, 44
Kerry, John, 75
Khalilzad, Zalmay, 65
Kim Jong-un, 82
King, Steve, 13, 20, 97
Knotts, Don, 198
Kogan, Aleksandr, 136, 137
Kovaleski, Serge, 185
Kudlow, Larry, 180, 182
Kushner, Jared, 49, 59, 109, 110, 111, 112, 131, 142, 182

Lamb, Conor, 185
Lee, Dr. Bandy, 148
Lewis, Sinclair, 84
Little, Patrick, 96
Lockwood, Ingersoll, 203
Macri, Mauricio, 114, 115
Macron, Emmanuel, 175, 181
Maduro, Nicolas, 54, 71
Manafort, Paul, 75, 76, 129, 142
Manigault-Newman, Omarosa, 36, 147, 170, 176
Mar-a-Lago, 68, 100, 116, 199
Marks, Lana, 57, 58
Martinelli, Ricardo, 114, 115
Masso, Edward "Sonny", 67
Mattis, James, 50, 168, 174, 175
May, Theresa, 178, 182
McCabe, Andrew, 113, 159
McCarthy, Joseph, 39, 211
McCarthy, Kevin
   The actor, not the GOP buffoon, 211
McConnell, Mitch, 27
McFly, Marty, 202
Meadows, Mark, 13, 19
Merkel, Angela, 182
Messer, Luke, 13, 14, 15
Miller, Stephen, 21, 30, 51, 123, 182, 192
Mnuchin, Steve, 126, 127
Mottley, Mia, 164

Mueller, Robert, 40, 59, 65, 75, 76, 78, 111, 113, 114, 116, 147, 159, 176, 208
Mulvaney, Mick, 127, 128
Mussolini, Benito, 23, 24
National Aeronautics and Space Administration, 34, 206
National Economic Council, 180
National Rifle Association, 208
Nehlen, Paul, 96
Netanyahu, Binyamin, 48, 49, 50
Nicholson, Jack, 81
Nielsen, Kirstjen, 198
Niinisto, Sauli, 60, 61
Nix, Alexander, 163
Nixon, Richard, 45, 113, 114, 145, 158, 160
Nunes, Devin, 40, 98
O'Malley, Martin, 185
Obama, Barack, 156, 158, 160, 161, 183
Odebrecht, 114, 115
Ohr, Bruce, 159
Pell, George, 120
Pence, Mike, 9, 25, 26, 37, 133, 167
Perdue, Sonny, 128
Perkins, Tony, 9, 56
Pompeo, Mike, 51, 123, 124, 126, 170
Price, Tom, 127
Prince, Erik, 36, 65, 137

Pruitt, Scott, 35, 118, 119, 120, 121
Queeg, Philip Francis, 144, 145
Quisling, Vidkun, 14
Rich, Seth, 140
Ripper, General Jack, 173
Roberts, Cokie, 185
Roberts, John, 28, 29, 186
Roosevelt, Franklin, 39, 82, 165, 178
Rosenstein, Rod, 113, 147, 149, 185
Ross, Wilbur, 129, 130
Rossello, Ricardo, 191, 194
Rouhani, Hassan, 74
Ryan, Paul, 17
Rybolovlev, Dmitry, 130, 131, 141
Sanders, Sarah Huckabee, 50, 159, 160
Sandler, Adam, 166
Satterfield, David, 64, 65, 67
Schiff, Adam, 184
Schumer, Chuck, 184
Schwarzenegger, Arnold, 7, 8
Sellers, Peter, 63, 173
Serling, Rod, 202, 208, 209, 210
Sessions, Jeff, 22, 39, 40, 185
Shine, Bill, 150
Shortey, Ralph, 120, 121
Silvers, Phil, 126
Smith, Peter W., 140

SPECTRE, 135, 141
Spencer, Richard, 21, 122, 192
Spicer, Sean, 30
Stadtmauer, Richard, 110, 111, 112
Stewart, Corey, 96
Stewart, Jimmy, 26
Stone, Roger, 48
Sträche, Heinz-Christian, 20
Strzok, Peter, 159
Sulzberger, A. G., 93, 94
Tannen, Biff, 202, 203
Thomas, Clarence, 42
THRUSH, 66
Tillerson, Rex, 123, 166, 167, 168, 169, 170
Trudeau, Justin, 180, 181, 182
Trump, Donald, 6, 13, 17, 23, 25, 40, 45, 46, 58, 85, 109, 112, 115, 135, 144, 148, 154, 159, 166, 167, 190, 202
Trump, Fred, 6, 101, 203
Trump, Ivanka, 109, 110, 111, 115, 116
Trump, Melania, 80, 171, 172
Turnbull, Malcolm, 183
Twilight Zone, 202, 208, 209, 212
U.S. Space Force, 206
Uribe, Alvaro, 115, 116
Vidal, Gore, 45
Warren, Elizabeth, 184
Waters, Maxine, 161, 184

West, Kanye, 204
West, Steve, 97
Wheeler, Andrew, 121
Whitaker, Matthew, 106, 184
Whitefish Energy, 192
Wilders, Geert, 20
Williams, Armstrong, 118
Wilson, Frederica, 184
Windrip, Buzz, 84, 85
Wolff, Michael, 167
Woodward, Bob, 50, 51, 130, 145, 172, 174, 175, 176, 180, 185
Wylie, Christopher, 136
Yates, Sally, 158, 159
Yiannopoulos, Milo, 98
Zinke, Ryan, 121, 122, 192